MANY SMOKES, MANY MOONS

A Chronology of American Indian History Through Indian Art

Photograph by N. J. Parrino courtesy of Cities Service Company

Ancient rock art on a canyon wall in the area of Vernal, Utah, depicts a hunting ritual.

AMERICAN INDIAN
TRIBES and CULTURES

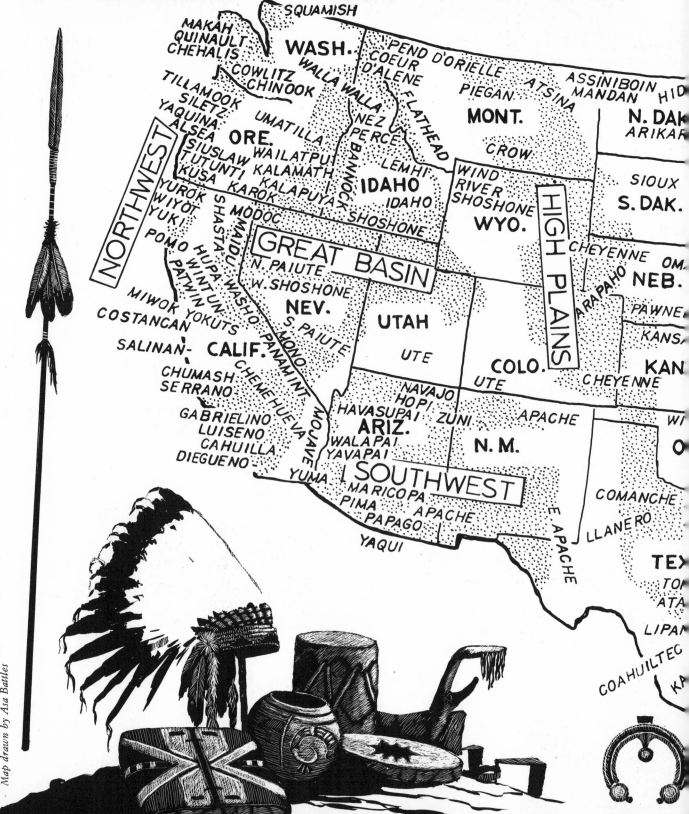

SQUAMISH

MAKAH
QUINAULT
CHEHALIS

WASH.

PEND D'ORIELLE
COEUR
D'ALENE

ASSINIBOIN
MANDAN
HID

COWLITZ
CHINOOK

WALLA WALLA

ATSINA

N. DAK

ARIKAR

TILLAMOOK
SILETZ
YAQUINA
ALSEA
SIUSLAW
TUTUNTI
KUSA

UMATILLA

ORE.

WAILATPU
KALAMATH
KALAPUYA
KAROK

NEZ
PERCE

FLATHEAD

PIEGAN

MONT.

CROW

LEMHI

WIND
RIVER
SHOSHONE

SIOUX
S. DAK.

BANNOCK

IDAHO

IDAHO

WYO.

YUROK
WIYOT
YUKI

SHASTA
MODOC
MAIDU
WASHO

NORTHWEST

POMO
HUPA
WINTUN
PATWIN

GREAT BASIN

N. PAIUTE
W. SHOSHONE

HIGH PLAINS

CHEYENNE OM.

MIWOK
COSTANCAN

YOKUTS
MONO
PANAMINT

NEV.

S. PAIUTE

UTAH

ARAPAHO
NEB.

PAWNE

SALINAN

CALIF.

UTE

KANS.

CHUMASH
SERRANO

CHEMEHUEVA
MOJAVE

COLO.

UTE

CHEYENNE

KAN

GABRIELINO
LUISENO
CAHUILLA
DIEGUENO

NAVAJO
HOPI
HAVASUPAI
ZUNI

APACHE

WI

WALAPAI
YAVAPAI

ARIZ.

N. M.

O

YUMA
MARICOPA
PIMA
PAPAGO

SOUTHWEST

COMANCHE

APACHE

E APACHE

LLANERO

YAQUI

TEX

TO
ATA

LIPAN

COAHUILTEC

KA

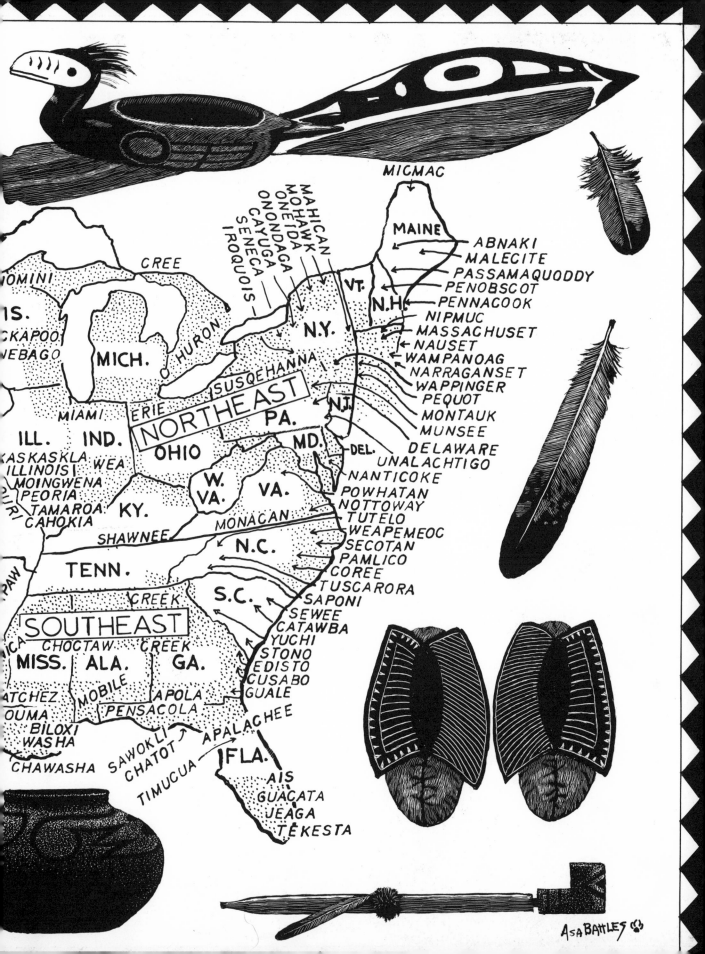

MICMAC

MAINE

MAHICAN
MOHAWK
ONEIDA
ONONDAGA
CAYUGA
SENECA
IROQUOIS

CREE

ABNAKI
MALECITE
PASSAMAQUODDY
PENOBSCOT
PENNACOOK
NIPMUC
MASSACHUSET
NAUSET
WAMPANOAG
NARRAGANSET
WAPPINGER
PEQUOT
MONTAUK
MUNSEE
DELAWARE
UNALACHTIGO
NANTICOKE
POWHATAN
NOTTOWAY
TUTELO
WEAPEMEOC
SECOTAN
PAMLICO
COREE
TUSCARORA
SAPONI
SEWEE
CATAWBA
YUCHI
STONO
EDISTO
CUSABO
GUALE

VT.
N.H.
N.Y.
N.J.
DEL.

MOMINI
IS.
CKAPOO
EBAGO
MICH.
ERIE
HURON
MIAMI
SUSQEHANNA
NORTHEAST
PA.
MD.
ILL.
IND.
OHIO
VA.
KASKASKIA
WEA
ILLINOIS
MOINGWENA
PEORIA
TAMAROA
CAHOKIA
KY.
W. VA.
MONACAN
SHAWNEE
N.C.
TENN.
S.C.
CREEK
SOUTHEAST
CHOCTAW
CREEK
MISS.
ALA.
GA.
ATCHEZ
MOBILE
APOLA
OUMA
PENSACOLA
BILOXI
WASHA
SAWOKLI
CHATOT
APALACHEE
CHAWASHA
TIMUCUA
FLA.
AIS
GUACATA
JEAGA
TEKESTA

AsaBattles

MANY SMOKES, MANY MOONS

A Chronology of American Indian History Through Indian Art

JAMAKE HIGHWATER

J. B. LIPPINCOTT COMPANY

PHILADELPHIA AND NEW YORK

U.S. LIBRARY OF CONGRESS CATALOGING IN PUBLICATION DATA

HIGHWATER, JAMAKE.
    MANY SMOKES, MANY MOONS.

    BIBLIOGRAPHY: P.
    INCLUDES INDEX.
    SUMMARY: WITH EMPHASIS ON THE TRIBES IN NORTH AMERICA, USES
THE ART AND ARTIFACTS OF VARIOUS INDIAN CULTURES TO ILLUSTRATE
EVENTS AFFECTING THEIR HISTORY FROM EARLIEST TIMES THROUGH 1973.
    1. INDIANS OF NORTH AMERICA—HISTORY—JUVENILE LITERATURE.
2. INDIANS OF NORTH AMERICA—ART—JUVENILE LITERATURE. [1. IN-
DIANS OF NORTH AMERICA—HISTORY. 2. INDIANS OF NORTH AMERICA—
ART] I. TITLE.
E77.4.H53   970′.004′97   77-17475   ISBN-0-397-31781-6

FOR ANDREW JACKSON

There will remain,
somewhere so deep within your ear
that it is called the mind,
the outcry of fleeing
Indians.

This will remain,
so deep within your hearing
that you will suffer
knowing
you alone can hear it.

—JAMAKE HIGHWATER

ACKNOWLEDGMENTS

The unique illustrations for this book were made possible through the generosity of numerous artists and institutions, and I wish to express my appreciation for their cooperation. I also wish to call attention to the names of these sources of the art for this book, which are printed next to the illustrations.

I have had the special pleasure and satisfaction of having two of my books designed by Jean Krulis, and I want to praise her uncommon artistry in interpreting my ideas for Many Smokes, Many Moons. *I am also deeply grateful to my loyal research assistant, Ken Seggerman, who made heroic efforts in helping to secure the illustrations.*

Finally, I hope to convey something of my affection and respect for J. B. Lippincott's editor-in-chief of books for young readers, Dorothy Briley. It is her vision that has allowed me to produce two of my favorite books—books that speak in the most intimate metaphors of both my personal ideas and those of my Indian ancestors.

JAMAKE HIGHWATER

PREFACE: ONE LAND, TWO WORLDS

When I was five years old, I discovered a wonderful creature. It looked like a bird, but it was able to do things that many other birds cannot do. For instance, in addition to flying in the enormous sky that shelters the land where I grew up, it swam and dove in the lakes and, sometimes, it just floated majestically on the water's silver surface. It could also waddle, rather gracelessly, in the tall grass that grew along the edges of the water. The bird was called *méksikatsi,* which, in the Blackfeet language, means "pink-colored feet." Méksikatsi seemed an ideal name for the versatile fly-swim bird, since it really did have bright pink feet.

When I was ten years old I was told by a teacher of the English language that *méksikatsi* was not really *méksikatsi.* It didn't matter that the word described the bird exactly or that the Blackfeet people had called it Méksikatsi for thousands of years. The bird, I was told, was called duck.

"DUCK?" I was extremely disappointed. The word "duck" didn't make any sense, for indeed Méksikatsi doesn't look like the word "duck." It doesn't even *sound* like the word "duck." So why do people call it duck?

This lesson was the first of many from which I slowly learned, to my amazement, that the people of white America don't *see* the same things that Indians see. America is one land, but it is two worlds.

As my education in the ways of white people progressed, I finally came to understand what duck means to them—but I could never forget that *méksikatsi* also has meaning, even though it means something *fundamentally* different from what duck means.

This lesson in words and the ideas they convey is very difficult to under-stand. In fact, it has been the most complicated lesson of my life. As I have gained more education in both the culture of the white man and that of the Indian, I have found it progressively more difficult to pass from one world to the other. It is not simply a matter of language, for, as everyone knows, it is possible to translate with accuracy from one language to another without losing too much of the original meaning. But there is no method for translating "alien ideas."

I am sometimes alienated by the way ideas find their way into English words. For instance, when an English word is descriptive—like the word "wilderness"—I am often appalled by what is implied by the description. After all, the forest is not "wild" in the sense that it is something that needs to be tamed. For Blackfeet Indians, the forest is the natural state of the world. It is the cities that are wild and need "taming." In a word like "universe" I find even more complicated problems, for Indians do not believe in a "*uni*-verse," but in a "*multi*-verse." Indians don't believe that there is only *one* truth, but think there are many truths.

I talked to my Indian friends at college about this situation, and we all agreed that it ought to be studied and understood by all people, because it surely contained a lesson that could benefit everybody.

If we can accept the paradox that the real humanity of people is under-stood through cultural *differences* rather than cultural similarities, then we can make profound sense of our differences. It is possible that there is not one truth, but many; not one *real* experience, but many realities; not one history, but many different ways of looking at events.

At the core of each person's life is a package of beliefs that he or she learns and that has been culturally determined long in advance of the person's birth. That is equally true for Indians and for white people. The world is made coherent by our description of it. Language permits us to express ourselves, but it also places limits on what we are able to say. What we call things largely determines how we evaluate them. What we see when we speak of "reality" is simply that preconception—that cultural package we inherited at birth. For me it was *méksikatsi;* for an English-speaking child it was duck. In-dian children are urged to see things and to name them in terms of the cultural package of the white man, but the children of white America are rarely given the opportunity to know the world as others know it.

I have become determined to clarify that Indians have a different way of looking at the world than white people do, and that that difference is *not* necessarily a matter of "error" or simply a variation in the words used to name things.

I discovered a sixteenth-century anonymous engraving that represented Columbus being greeted "by natives of the dominion of the Great Khan." I asked Choctaw Indian artist Asa Battles to make a drawing of the same event from the Indian perspective.

The old engraving depicts three sailing vessels anchored offshore and a landing party of elegantly dressed gentlemen erecting a cross on the new-found land while their leader, Columbus, flanked by two officers, is given a rich tribute by natives who do not look in the least like Indians. It is a familiar depiction of a famous scene from the white man's idealized history.

Courtesy of the Library of Congress

The other picture depicts an unfamiliar scene: an Indian gasping in amazement as a floating island carrying odd creatures with hairy faces and tall defoliated trees approaches.

Drawing by Asa Battles

When I showed the two pictures to white people they said, "Well, of course you realize that what those Indians thought they saw—if you *really* investigate the facts—was not really there at all." In other words, there were no island and no defoliated trees, but a ship with a party of Spaniards.

Indians, looking at the same pictures, pause with perplexity and then say, "Well, after all, a ship is a floating island, and what are the masts of a ship but the trunks of tall trees?" In other words, what the Indians saw was real in terms of their own experience.

The artists of all races have known for years that "reality" depends on how you look at things. An Indian teacher has said it in another way: "The apple is very complicated, but for the apple tree it is easy."

The Indians saw a floating island while white men saw a ship. Isn't it also possible—if we use our imaginations—that another, more alien people with an utterly different way of seeing and thinking might see neither an island nor a ship? They might see the complex network of molecules that science tells us produce the outward shapes and colors that we *see* as objects. In that case, who *really* sees "reality"?

We see the world in terms of our cultural heritage. Among politically concerned people with a liberal dogma, there is a good-natured and pompous insistence that all people are fundamentally the same. What is *fundamental,* however, to people concerned with political idealism is sometimes rather superficial. Some libertarians seem to believe that even biology is democratic, but what they see when they refer to the homogeneous attributes of all human physiology is not blood or nerves, but things that are much more cultural. They do not like to notice that races and national groups tend to evolve distinctive stereotypes both emotionally and physically. They believe that *all* men are fundamentally the same because all men—they insist—need and want the same things. They do not take into consideration the reason a Navajo family may rip the toilet out of its newly built government house. Navajos believe it is disgusting to put a toilet under the same roof with people rather than at a distance from the house. Many liberals also fail to take into account the great variety of ways in which people of a single culture respond to the same things, let alone the vaster differences that exist between cultures. There is no question that all people feel sorrow and happiness, but the things that evoke these responses and the manner in which such feelings may be expressed socially can be highly dissimilar from culture to culture.

Political idealists have overemphasized the uniformity of people. It is exceedingly dangerous to take democratic idealism out of politics and attempt to apply it to science and art. The *uniformity* that the biologist and physicist discover at the core of the material world is easily distorted into *conformity* when applied to less fundamental issues, and gradually we find that the very democratic process that is supposed to set us free has deprived cultures and individuals of the right to be dissimilar.

It is very unfashionable at the moment to suggest that all people are *not* the same. It is equally unpopular to insist that we can learn more about a culture from its differences than from its similarities to other cultures, and that the basis of human nature is probably more visible in human diversity than in the relatively few ways in which we are fundamentally the same. Political people usually strive for admirable but naïve political goals: one nation, one world. In the process of trying to unify the world we must be exceedingly careful not to destroy the diversity of the many cultures of man that give human life meaning, focus, and vitality.

I grew up in two Americas—the ancient one that existed for my ancestors for tens of thousands of years, and the new one that is written about in history books. Like the pictures of the Spanish landing, the tales of these two Americas are rarely compatible. It is for this reason that the arts of American Indians are precious—they provide a glimpse into their own history, into the world of the *other* America.

For a long time the viewpoint of primal peoples, such as Indians, was considered naïve and primitive, especially if the peoples kept their history alive through oral and pictorial traditions rather than by writing history books. Today we are learning that people are not the same, and that we cannot evaluate all experience the same way. We are also learning that everybody doesn't have to be the same in order to be equal. It is no longer realistic for dominant cultures to send out missionaries to convert everyone to their ideas of the "truth." Today we are beginning to look into the ideas of groups outside the dominant culture, and we are finding different kinds of "truth" that make the world we live in far bigger than we ever dreamed it could be—for the greatest distance between people is not geographical space, but culture. This book is an effort to make bridges across the vast spaces between Indians and non-Indians and to explore the America of native Americans as it is made visible through Indian art.

A NOTE ABOUT TIME, SCIENCE, AND THE ILLUSTRATIONS IN THIS BOOK

There is a lively controversy among archaeologists and anthropologists over the dates of various major events in pre-Columbian America, particularly the dates ascribed to ancient archaeological finds. They also dispute the reliability of the various methods used to determine when these ancient objects were produced by the people of America. I have taken a somewhat liberal stand in the matter of dates, avoiding the extremes of both the very conservative (who tend to think of man's residency in America as rather recent) and the very radical (who believe that man has been in America far longer than prior generations of scientists imagined). There is among Indians, of course, an inclination to accept the views of those who consider American culture to be very ancient, since those views coincide with what folk histories tell Indians about the origins of their world.

This chronology of America's Indians is a selective overview of events, and concentrates on events that pertain both to history and to culture. In dealing with early periods, before the coming of the white man, I have treated the Americas as a single unit. But where events in post-Columbian times become politically diversified and localized, I have focused attention on North America.

Most illustrated Indian histories are written by non-Indians and rely heavily upon the art of non-Indians. It has been my aim in this book to use only Indian art and artifacts to illustrate the viewpoint of Indians themselves in regard to major cultural, political, and military events in America.

THE DAWN
OF AMERICA

At the place where all things began, there was at first the Black World.
Living there, among the spirits, were First Man and First Woman, and the
famous trickster called Coyote. The First World was a rock in a sea of mist,
and it was not a good place. The beings of that dark world made war on each
other, and so the spirits and creatures fled through an opening in the East
into the Blue World, which was the Second World. But with them they took
the evils of the First World.

*Drawing by Raymond Johnson courtesy of the
Navajo Community College, Navajo Nation*

When First Man and First Woman and Coyote climbed to the Blue World, they found Sun and Moon and a misty light. Sun tried to make love to First Woman and there was great trouble. Coyote, who knows everything, called the spirits and they sat together and they spoke. After many speeches, they decided that the Second World was too small and that its inhabitants would have to ascend into the Third World, where there would be room enough for Sun to shine in a distant place, separated from First Woman forever. This Third World was called the Yellow World and was a place of beauty. The people living in this world welcomed the newcomers who climbed from the Blue World, but they gave warning that it would not be good to anger the water monster called Tieholtsodi. Coyote, however, was always very curious, and he ignored the warning and went to the eastern waters, where he found two of the children of Tieholtsodi. They were so beautiful that Coyote captured them and hid them in his blanket.

Painting by Andrew Tsinahjinnie courtesy of the Navajo Curriculum Center, Navajo Nation

Soon the four oceans surged and the tide rose among the mountains. The water monster was enraged, for he could not find his children, and his tears poured over the land.

To escape the flood, the people piled the Four Mountains of the Yellow World one upon the other, but still the water rose dangerously. So the people planted a giant reed on the top of the sacred mountains and it began to grow. When the reed had reached the yellow sky, it pierced a hole into the Fourth World. The ancestors of all people and all animals and all spirits followed First Man and First Woman and Coyote into the center of the reed and climbed into the world above.

The Fourth World was large and filled by the flowing of three great misty lights, dimmed now and again by the coming down of darkness. First Man and First Woman arranged the Four Mountains, and in the central plain there began to flow a vast river. On the north bank lived human people, and on the south bank lived all the people in the form of animals. It was a good world, but there was no peace, for Coyote still possessed the children of the water monster and the sea continued to rise until the new world became soft under the people's feet, and finally the flood burst through the ground and the water rose against them. Again they piled the mountains one atop the other and again a reed was planted and grew to the sky that hung above the Fourth World. At last the way was opened for the people into the Fifth World, where they hoped to be safe at last. Each person carried a bundle of his or her best things, hoping to take them to safety.

But still the waters pursued them until, suddenly, the horns of Tieholtsodi appeared in the midst of the new land and the people became very frightened and they trembled. They came together like children and each revealed the precious contents of his or her bundle so the water monster would know that none of the people was a thief. When it came Coyote's turn to open his blanket, he was forced to reveal the stolen children. The people understood their troubles and quickly returned the children to their angry parent. And then the monster and his children went away and the waters that had arisen receded into the underworlds, and the land became firm again.

At the Place of Emergence the people named themselves Diné, which means "the people." Later they became known as "the Navajo people"—they were named this countless years later by the strangers who came from the sea.

The story of First Man and First Woman and Coyote is the story of the Creation according to the history of the Navajo people. They tell us they are "the original people" of America, and that all other tribes descended from them and went off to build their own villages and to create their own languages in the era, very long ago, before the destruction of a tribe of monsters by the Warrior Twins.

There are many histories of America. It is a land rich in the mythic and archaeological relics of a vast, still mysterious past. Abandoned and eroded, the most ancient works of Indians evoked wild speculation among the first European explorers. The white men invented myths of their own—about Lost Tribes of Israel that had found their way to the western hemisphere; about survivors from the sunken continents of Atlantis and Mu; and about an extinct superrace, the Mound Builders, that had raised the great earthworks that confounded the white settlers of eastern America. Gradually the scientists who read the rocks discovered another history of America. That story, which is summarized in this book, ran virtually uninterrupted from at least 15,000 B.C. to the twentieth century A.D.

c. 35,000–15,000 B.C.

The first waves of a distinctive people of Asiatic affinity—today collectively called Paleo-Indians—arrived in the western hemisphere by crossing a vast ice bridge from Siberia to Alaska; this ice bridge formed in the Bering Strait because of the lowering of the sea level caused by massive glaciation. These first immigrants discovered a huge land mass rolling from the frozen ice cap in the extreme north to the lush tropics of Florida. Its vast spaces offered few barriers to the journeys of the ancient nomadic hunters, who came, before the invention of the wheel or the formation of contemporary languages, into this immense, silent place to become the first Americans—they who truly discovered America.

c. 28,000 B.C.

The first Americans were hunters of great mammals who lived during the Wisconsin glacial period of the Pleistocene Epoch (the Ice Age). Possibly the earliest artifact rediscovered so far is a six-inch-long fragment of mastodon pelvic bone unearthed by Mexican anthropologist Juan Armentia Camacho near Puebla, Mexico, in 1959. It is scratched with the likenesses of camels, tapirs, mastodons, and other animals now extinct in North America, and it is believed to have been carved when the bone was fresh.

The fragment of mastodon pelvic bone found near Puebla, Mexico, by anthropologist Juan Armentia Camacho.

Courtesy of Dr. Juan Armentia Camacho

c. 18,000–7000 B.C.

The spear points used by Paleo-Indian hunters were chipped from stone. (Metallurgy was virtually unknown in North America until 1492.) The points have been found in buried heaps of bones from animals killed by the hunters, and they are named for the sites where they were first discovered. Sandia points, for instance, were originally found in a New Mexico cave—though they were subsequently also located in most parts of the American continents. Sandia points were made perhaps as early as twenty thousand years ago. The Clovis (New Mexico) point is usually thought to have been invented about twelve thousand years ago, while Folsom (New Mexico) points were made by Ice Age buffalo hunters perhaps ten thousand years ago.

STAGES AND CULTURES	APPROX. DATES	PRIMARY GAME HUNTED	PROJECTILE POINTS
PLANO	9,500 TO 7,000 YEARS AGO	PRONGHORN ANTELOPE, MODERN BISON, BIGHORN BISON	
PLAINVIEW	10,000 TO 7,500 YEARS AGO	BIGHORN BISON	
FOLSOM	11,000 TO 9,000 YEARS AGO	BIGHORN BISON	
LLANO	15,000 TO 11,000 YEARS AGO	MAMMOTH	
SANDIA	25,000 TO 12,000 YEARS AGO	BIGHORN BISON, HORSE, MAMMOTH, CAMEL	
PRE-PROJECTILE STAGES	38,000 TO 20,000 YEARS AGO	SABERTOOTH, MAMMOTH, DIRE WOLF	SCRAPERS

Drawing by Asa Battles

AsaBattles

c. 9000 B.C.

The Pleistocene Epoch or Ice Age ended, and suddenly many animals became extinct; this deprived early man of bountiful game. Native American mammals began to become extinct twelve thousand years ago, and species continued to die out for six thousand years. (Not since the dinosaurs became extinct sixty-five million years ago have so many species vanished so suddenly and dramatically.) Woolly mammoths vanished in 8000 B.C.; tapirs and ground sloths disappeared in 7500 B.C.; bighorn bison became extinct in 6500 B.C.; and native horses, camels, and giant armadillos were gone by 5500 B.C. Although mammals died out in other parts of the world, the major extinctions occurred in North America. Paul Martin of the University of Arizona insists that early man was a major cause of the North American extinctions. New hunting technology, Martin says, made overkill possible.

c. 9000 B.C.

The first traces of the Desert Culture of the Great Basin of North America were left by hunter-gatherers who occupied Danger Cave, which overlooks the Great Salt Desert in western Utah. The Desert Culture eventually became a major Indian life-style.

c. 8000 B.C.

In Tierra del Fuego, off the southern tip of South America, men living in caves continued to hunt giant ground sloths with weapons of chipped stone.

c. 7500 B.C.

Ancient people of the Andes made campsites at Lauricocha in the central Peruvian highlands.

c. 7500 B.C.

At Danger Cave, Utah, where evidence of a thriving Desert Culture was found, baskets were made by the rudimentary technique called twining.

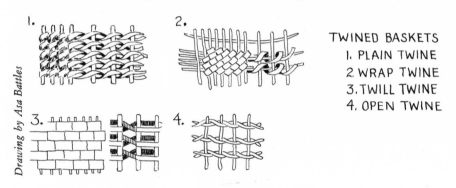

Drawing by Asa Battles

TWINED BASKETS
1. PLAIN TWINE
2. WRAP TWINE
3. TWILL TWINE
4. OPEN TWINE

c. 7000 B.C.

With the decline of Ice Age hunters, the new Desert Culture spread widely. The shift from a life-style focused on big game to one based on the use of a variety of plant and animal foods was a central part of the stage of North American history called the Archaic, which reached its height some seven thousand years ago. The new, broader economy depended on foraging, rather than hunting.

Many great technological leaps seem to have taken place about nine thousand years ago. Among the finds made in Danger Cave, on the western edge of the Great Salt Desert in Utah, are remnants of coiled cords that are almost certain indications that the people of Danger Cave knew how to weave baskets—the ideal, lightweight containers for a foraging people. In the opinion of some experts, the inhabitants of Danger Cave were the first people in the entire world to master this enormously important skill.

Nearly one hundred sandals woven from shredded sagebrush bark have been found in Fort Rock Cave in south-central Oregon; according to radiocarbon dating tests, they are about nine thousand years old.

Courtesy of L. S. Cressman

Sandals found in Fort Rock Cave, Oregon.

c. 7000 B.C.

In California and Baja California, the Pinto Basin Culture dominated the Far West. This culture was based on an economy of fish and shellfish.

c. 6000 B.C.

Geological changes prevented salmon from migrating up the Columbia River to their spawning grounds. With the disappearance of the once plentiful fish, the Indians in the Northwest found it necessary to adopt a gathering-hunting life-style.

c. 5000 B.C.

In California, a Desert Culture developed at Lake Mojave and San Dieguito, where food-grinding implements were in use. The culture was also found in La Jolla, south of Los Angeles.

c. 5000–3000 B.C.

Maize (corn) was domesticated in the Tehuacan Valley of the south-central highlands of Mexico. Also domesticated were beans, chili peppers, and other food plants. This set the stage for widespread agricultural and sedentary village life.

c. 3000 B.C.

Remnants of the earliest pottery have been dated to this period. There is a controversy over whether pottery was invented independently in the Americas, or was introduced by outsiders. G. Ekholm has been a leading exponent of theories of pre-Columbian contacts between the Americas and other continents, and it is possible that pottery-making skills were taught to American Indians by immigrants from Asia. The earliest pottery found anywhere in the Americas dates from about six thousand to five thousand years ago and has been found in the areas of Monagrillo in Panama and around Valdivia on the coast of Ecuador. Its distinctive designs and decorations do not seem to exist anyplace else in the world except in the Jomon Culture on Kyushu, the southernmost island of Japan—and the dates for this specific kind of pottery are about the same in both places. No archaeologist has found a way of explaining what Japanese pottery is doing on the coast of Ecuador, nor how such sophisticated pottery could arise quite suddenly in Ecuador, as it seems to have done. There are no known examples of previous, amateurish attempts at pottery making.

Recently archaeologists have determined that the Chalco pottery found in remains on the Hondo River, near Mexico City, is among the old known examples of American pottery. The Chalco pottery dates to about 4500 B.C.

Valdivia "Dog Bone" design.

Valdivia fine drag-jab punctation.

Jomon broad-line incised design.

Jomon heavy drag-jab punctation.

Drawing by Asa Battles

c. 3000 B.C.

Two important northern Woodland cultures began: the culture of the Red Paint People, so called because the farmers who first found their burial pits noted the linings of bright red hematite, perhaps a symbol of blood and life; and the Old Copper Archaic Culture, taking its name from the copper objects that the Indians produced by hammering pure copper nuggets.

c. 2600 B.C.

According to archaeologist Norman Hammond, excavations in Belize (British Honduras) in Central America have pushed back the origins of the Maya to 2600 to 2500 B.C. The buildings and pottery uncovered clearly foreshadow the splendor of the Classic Maya period, and also seem to predate the Olmec, which is often thought to have produced the "mother culture" of the region that invented and passed on many of the characteristics of Mesoamerican culture.

c. 2500 B.C.

Courtesy of the Arizona State Museum

A split-twig deer, one of many found since 1933 in almost inaccessible caves in Arizona's Grand Canyon, dates from this period and is thought to have been a talisman used by early man in America to ensure successful hunts.

A split-twig deer found in the Grand Canyon.

c. 2000 B.C.

The ancestors of the people who eventually became known as the Maya populated a vast region of some one hundred twenty-five thousand square miles in Guatemala, western Honduras, Belize (British Honduras), and the Mexican states of Yucatan, Compeche, Tabasco, eastern Chiapas, and Tuintana Roo.

c. 2000–1500 B.C.

The Indians of Florida and Georgia began making fired earthenware ceramics. Undecorated pottery that dates from this period was found in 1933–41 at Ocmulgee Mounds, east of Macon, Georgia. The creation and use of pottery gradually became a central cultural activity of many North American Indian tribes.

c. 1500 B.C.

Ancient silver figurines by Inca artists of the alpaca (left) and the llama.

Courtesy of the American Museum of Natural History

Small tribal communities began to appear in the central Andes on the north and central coasts of Peru. By 900 B.C. farmers of the region began to use irrigation and to domesticate the llama—the only native American pack animal besides the dog. Goldsmithing was also practiced locally.

c. 1500 B.C.

Towns of considerable size throughout Mexico and Guatemala were the results of economies based on extensive agriculture. The dog had probably been domesticated by this time in Central and North America.

c. 1200 B.C.

The Olmec, the first known settlers of the Valley of Mexico, left debris on the shore of Lake Texacoco at Ayotla, and buried their dead on the western side of the lake at Tlatilco. In the highlands of Guatemala, earthen platforms (pyramidal mounds) were being used as altars or funeral monuments by the ancestors of the Maya.

c. 1000 B.C.

An Indian "artist" painted the walls of a cave in the Pecos River area of Texas. The pictographic art shows elongated shamans (holy men) invoking the power of the hunt. The large figure carries prickly-pear pouches containing hunting implements, and holds arrows or spears in one hand and an atlatl (a spear-launching device) in the other. Deer—some of them wounded—race across the bottom of the painting toward the other shaman, who is armed with weapons.

Courtesy of the Texas Memorial Museum; watercolor reproduction by Forrest Kirkland

A rock painting from Panther Cave in the Pecos River Valley.

c. 1000–300 B.C.

Mysterious Serpent Mound built by the Adena people.

Courtesy of the Ohio Historical Society

The Adena Culture gradually reached its highest achievement in southern Ohio, northern Kentucky, and the surrounding region. Beginning in about 1000 B.C., a forest people of the Ohio Valley began building burial mounds by heaping basketloads of earth over the log-lined tombs of their elite. Another characteristic of their culture was cord- or fabric-impressed pottery and perhaps, even at the period of their earliest activity, the domestication of plants. The Adena preoccupation with death and with an art of stylized animal forms found a more elaborate expression in the Hopewell Culture, which overlapped and gradually replaced the Adena in the Ohio Valley; it began in about 300 B.C.

An Adena effigy pipe.

c. 1000 B.C.

On the Great Plains of North America the influence of the eastern Hopewell cult moved westward up river valleys, reaching the Rocky Mountains by the third century A.D. and briefly producing a flowering of the so-called Plains Woodland Culture. Though this culture had waned by 1000 A.D., its influence was probably responsible for the creation of permanent dwellings in the form of large, square pit houses covered with roofs of timber and earth—the first examples of the Plains lodge structure.

c. 1000 B.C.

The earliest traces of Coast Salish people were left on the Pacific Northwest Coast. This culture's economy was based on hunting large marine animals with toggle harpoons. At the same time, the ancestors of the Tsimshian people arrived on the lower Skeena River.

c. 1000 B.C.

The Olmec, one of the oldest and most influential of Central American Indian cultures, founded ceremonial centers in the Tabasco and Veracruz states of Mexico. La Venta, one of the major Olmec sites, is famous for its colossal sculptures of human heads. Why these heads have a "negroid" appearance has been a persistent mystery, for they were made long before black slaves were brought into the Americas from Africa. The Olmec were probably the first people to make use of the jaguar symbols that became a dominant image in the arts of Central America.

An Olmec head.

c. 600 B.C.

The early ancestors of the Maya left fragments of pottery on the bedrock that underlies the North Acropolis of the ceremonial center of Tikal, which was eventually built on this site in the Petén region of Guatemala.

c. 550 B.C.

In the Virú Valley of Peru, the first signs of large-scale irrigation and of complex fortifications in the Americas appeared at places such as the Castle of Tomaval, a vast terraced adobe structure resembling an apartment house.

300 B.C.–1400 A.D.

Ancestors of Arizona's Pima Indians—known by the Pima word "Hohokam," which means "those who have gone"—founded a distinctive culture, farming their desert lands with the use of extensive canal irrigation, producing corn, and gathering wild beans and cactus as food supplements. Slowly both Hohokam pottery and Hohokam basketry evolved into exceptional arts. Large ball courts like those used by the Maya of Central America for their sacred and not yet understood ball games were also found among many of the Hohokam villages; they were made of hard-packed earth.

An example of
Hohokam pottery.

Courtesy of the Arizona State Museum

c. 300 b.c.–300 a.d.

The people of the Hopewell Culture of Ohio, Illinois, and Wisconsin built large burial mounds and used exquisite carvings of animals and humans in pottery, mica, stone, and copper as funerary offerings.

Courtesy of the Ohio State Museum

A Hopewell frog effigy pipe.

c. 200 b.c.

The great civilization centered at Teotihuacán, northeast of Mexico City, began to develop. Within two hundred fifty years the city dominated the Valley of Mexico and overran the other cultures of Mexico, Central America, and the southwestern region of what became the United States.

c. 200 b.c.

In the northern coastal area of Peru, the Mochica Culture evolved a highly complex pre-Inca Andean civilization, originating an ideographic writing system and building canals and roads. The Mochica worshipped cats, and animals were central to both their religious and secular lives. They domesticated the dog, llama, and guinea pig. They used the blowgun for hunting and created a unique form of effigy pottery that many consider their most monumental cultural achievement.

A Mochica vessel.

C. 200 B.C.

A simple form of pottery originated in the Arctic. Pottery fragments that were found at Cape Denbigh, Alaska, have been dated to this period. The first inhabitants of the western Arctic are little known. Earliest were the Ice Age big-game hunters from northern Asia. Later came hunters of the Northwest Microblade Culture—Indians who used tiny stone blades. The culture of a subsequent people, which is known as the Arctic Small Tool Tradition and was characterized by delicately flaked implements, may have developed in Siberia. These people were probably the main ancestors of the contemporary Eskimo (Inuit), whose highly evolved use of resources enabled them to populate the entire Arctic.

This ink drawing on reindeer skin by Alaskan artist George Aghupuk depicts many activities of Arctic life.

c. 100 B.C.–500 A.D.

Aleuts gradually settled parts of the Alaskan Peninsula as well as the Aleutian Islands. They lived in pit houses made of driftwood and sod, and employed the weapon called the harpoon to hunt sea mammals and fish. They traveled on the sea in small boats made of animal skins stretched over wooden frames. At a later time the Aleuts built kayaks as well as large, open boats called umiaks.

c. 100 A.D.

In the Pacific Northwest there was a great increase in the use of heavy wood-working tools, particularly in the Fraser Delta. Probably the art of carving monumental cedar-log poles and posts and the construction of canoes and houses using cedar planks and logs began at this period.

c. 100–700 A.D.

The Indians of the upper Great Lakes region of North America discovered an almost pure form of copper that they fashioned by hammering and shaping into tools, ornaments, and utensils.

c. 100–700 A.D.

In Utah, Colorado, Arizona, and New Mexico a people known as the Basketmaker Indians lived by means of foraging and some farming. Basket making was highly developed among these people, for baskets provided an ideal, lightweight, flexible carrier for use in collecting wild plants and seeds. The early Basketmakers did not have pottery, but eventually their descendants learned to make pots of mud and dry them in the sun.

c. 400 A.D.

In southern Ohio, Illinois, and surrounding regions, vast earthworks were constructed by Indians of the highly evolved Hopewell Culture. These people derived much of their material culture from the earlier and faded Adena. In addition to burial mounds, typical Hopewell artifacts include excellent pottery, metalwork, and stonework. A wide variety of imported materials—obsidian, sheet mica, copper, pearls—were used in Hopewell mortuary art; such materials reached the Ohio Valley through an extensive trade network that stretched from the Rockies to the Atlantic and from the Great Lakes to the Gulf Coast. Hopewell culture also produced extensive geometric earthworks that presumably were used for ceremonial purposes.

Archaeological finds from this period include the remains of cremated dead and an astonishing range of tomb offerings. Corn, beans, and squash were

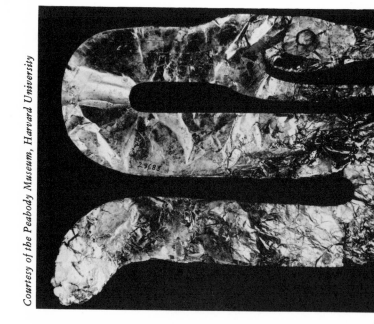

A Hopewell snake image made from mica.

cultivated, and other foods were obtained by gathering and hunting. The size of the burial mounds and earthworks suggests that Hopewell culture was supported by a large and complex population with a highly developed ceremonial life and religious hierarchy. Though Hopewell culture and influence disappeared by 700 A.D., its subsistence pattern of forest hunting and farming continued over most of the Northeast until European contact more than eight centuries later.

c. 400 A.D.

The great ceremonial center of the Maya Highlands, Kaminaljuyú, near Guatemala City, was overrun by the people of Teotihuacán in the Valley of Mexico, who had evolved to the height of their culture. The Classic Maya style and that of Teotihuacán blended during the next two hundred years, producing the Esperanza Culture. During this same time, the influence of Teotihuacán spread throughout the Maya world.

c. 500–1000 A.D.

Eskimo (Inuit) of the Birnirk Culture of northwestern Alaska and northeastern Siberia built houses of
sod and driftwood and carved realistic human figures
of ivory and wood. They lived by hunting and fishing, and by gathering birds' eggs, shellfish, roots, and
berries. A variety of weapons and tools were produced, including whalebone shovels and ivory snow
goggles. Transport was supplied by boats called
kayaks and umiaks, and by sleds.

An Eskimo ivory figurine.

*Courtesy of the Museum
of the American India*
Heye Foundation

c. 500 A.D.

The bow and arrow, which had been in use in Europe since 7000 B.C., finally
became widely used in America, replacing the atlatl, a spear-launching device
the name of which derives from the Aztec.

c. 500 A.D.

In the Northwest Coast area, a great emphasis upon wealth and social position
became well established and was the dominant focus of the cultures of the
region. At about the same time, the first burial mounds appeared in this area.

c. 550 A.D.

Tikal, one of the greatest Maya centers of its time, reached the height of its development, with an estimated population of more than forty-five thousand inhabiting a region of about twenty-five square miles. Tikal, located in Petén, Guatemala, was prosperous and powerful for almost three hundred years; during that time its five temple-pyramids and its many palaces, shrines, terraces, ball courts, steam baths, and ceremonial platforms were constructed. These structures were connected by four wide causeways paved with plaster and brightly painted.

One of Tikal's temple-pyramids.

c. 600 A.D.

Zapotec Indians inhabited the site of Monte Albán, Mexico, an arid district not well suited to the founding of a great ceremonial center. The Indians constructed a dam to preserve rainwater and developed the severe and massive style of architecture that characterizes much of the present ruins. The Zapotec were succeeded by the Mixtec at this site in about 900 A.D.

c. 650 A.D.

The culture of Teotihuacán, after a triumphant reign that reached far beyond the Valley of Mexico, collapsed. The population declined and the arts of its distinctive civilization decayed.

c. 700 A.D.

According to Maya tradition, the ceremonial center of Chichén Itzá was founded on the Yucatán Peninsula in 711.

c. 700 A.D.

Teotihuacán was destroyed and burned for reasons unknown; it is generally assumed that there was an invasion of nomadic Chichimec ("barbarians") from the north. Some of the buildings—the pyramids of the Sun and Moon, and the Temple Quetzalcóatl (the Feathered Serpent)—survived. The ruins remained a shrine of the Indians until the Spanish invasion in the sixteenth century. During this time a strong flow of Mexican cultural traits diffused to

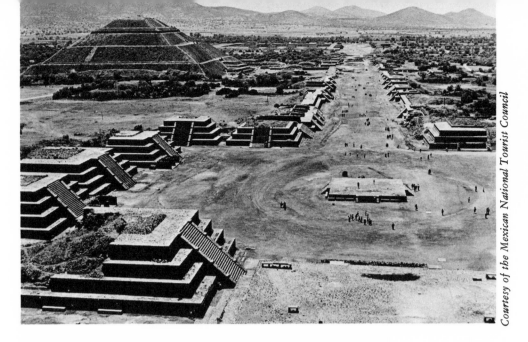

Courtesy of the Mexican National Tourist Council

Panoramic view of the ruins of Teotihuacán.

the Eastern Woodlands of North America. Temple mounds and painted pottery appeared and social structures called chiefdoms that were like those of the Mexicans developed for the first time in the Southeast. Cahokia, the largest settlement, reached a population of fifteen thousand. (Cahokia was located in what is now Illinois.)

c. 700 A.D.

A new life-style, rooted in agriculture, began in the southeastern part of North America. Named for the river valley along which it appears to have originated, Mississippian culture is characterized by elaborate pottery, flat-topped mounds arranged around open plazas, and rectangular thatch-roofed houses, all supposedly reflecting notable influences from Middle America. (Archaeologists do not by any means all agree that the Mississippian was influenced by Mesoamerican cultures.) To the north, a people who buried their dead in mounds that were sometimes in the shapes of birds or animals and sometimes dome-shaped lived in Wisconsin along the streams and lakes. These migratory hunters are called Effigy Mound Builders. In the South, fortified mound villages spread eastward along the Mississippi and its numerous tributaries all the way to the Atlantic. The ritualism of this Temple Mound Period (700–1700 A.D.) produced a vast body of ceremonial objects, including embossed sheet-copper plates, stone figures, long blades of flint, and engraved shell bowls.

A Mississippian head pot.

Courtesy of the University of Arkansas Museum

c. 700 A.D.

The Early Pueblo Period began, growing out of the earlier Hohokam and Mogollon cultures. The people of the Anasazi Culture (which flowered as early as 100 B.C.) abandoned the use of pit houses and began to construct above-ground houses, an architectural movement that culminated around 1000 A.D. in apartmentlike complexes of adobe and stone. Driven by drought from their Four Corners homeland about 1300 A.D., Pueblo farmers migrated southward and eastward, relocating at their present locations on the Rio Grande.

c. 800 A.D.

At a small Maya site called Bonampak, located in the Mexican state of Chiapas near the Guatemala border, artists painted the most renowned of remaining murals from the Late Classic period of Maya culture (450–750 A.D.). These

A section of the
Bonampak murals.

murals—brilliant, full-color wall paintings in three rooms of a small temple lost for centuries in the jungle—provide a rare insight into the court life of the Maya. Rediscovered in 1946, the murals appear to record a single narrative involving ritual preparations, a raid for sacrificial victims, and the rituals that followed the raid. The sometimes grotesque scenes suggest that the Maya were not as peaceful as archaeologists once thought. The murals are faded and greatly eroded by the climate of the jungle; however, excellent reproductions were made at the time of their rediscovery, and these are now in the collection of the Museum of Anthropology in Mexico City.

800-900 A.D.

Gradually the great Maya centers of the lowland (Petén) region of Guatemala declined. The people ceased to construct buildings and to sculpt monuments, which apparently bore important historical records and depicted the passage of time. (The passage of time was a subject that the Maya accorded the utmost seriousness and ceremonial attention.) From 800—when the exquisite center called Copán in Honduras was abandoned—to 889—when the last date was recorded on the stone pillars (stela) sculpted by the Maya—the lowland Maya centers, including great Tikal, were abandoned. The people, however, remained; they lived outside the ceremonial centers in rural villages. At some sites monuments were destroyed, and some construction was halted while in progress. There is currently no accepted explanation for the decline of the Maya world, but theories range from political revolution by unhappy "serfs" to the invasion of a non-Maya people.

c. 825 A.D.

The ancestors of the Apache began to break away from northern Athapaskan groups (located through the interior portions of Alaska and western Canada) and to drift southward.

c. 900 A.D.

A Náhuatl-speaking people called the Toltec founded a new empire that dominated a vast region of southern Mexico. Originally from the northwest of Mesoamerica, this people had a cultural and ethnic composition that appears to

These great carved warriors once supported a Toltec temple at Tula, near Mexico City.

have resulted from extensive exchanges and intermarriage with the various peoples of Mexico's centers of civilization. At its height, the Toltec empire had a population of about two hundred thousand inhabiting a highly centralized region. The capital was called Tula; it was located in Hidalgo state, Mexico, and was one of the prime ceremonial centers of Central America until it was destroyed by the Chichimec Indians in the twelfth century.

c. 987 A.D.

The Feathered Serpent, Quetzalcóatl Topiltzin, the first known leader of the Toltec, led his people away from Culhuacán, the old capital, which stood immediately to the south of what is now Mexico City, to the new Toltec capital, called Tula (the legendary Tollán of Aztec chronicles). About 987 a conflict between the followers of Quetzalcóatl and the militaristic followers of Tez-

Quetzalcóatl,
the Feathered Serpent.

From the Aztec Codex Magliabecchi,
Biblioteca Nazionale Centrale, Florence

catlipoca resulted in the exile of Quetzalcóatl Topiltzin, who sailed away on a raft into the sunrise across the Gulf of Mexico from what is now Veracruz, promising to return on the anniversary of the year of his birth. A similar tradition was known to the Maya of the Yucatán Peninsula; the Maya legend recounted the story of a man who arrived in Yucatán in 987 from the west (from the direction of present-day Veracruz) and took control of the peninsula, where he founded his capital at Chichén Itzá. His name was the Maya equivalent of the name of the Feathered Serpent—Kukulcán.

c. 1000 A.D.

Norsemen from northern Europe arrived in Newfoundland shortly after Eric the Red settled Greenland in 985. Newfoundland was the Vinland of the Norse sagas. It was abandoned a short time later.

c. 1000 A.D.

Mississippian culture was fully formed; it was concentrated along the Mississippi River and in the Southern Woodlands and was an elaborate death cult with a strong preoccupation with burial rites.

c. 1000 A.D.

The Hohokam Indians of southern Arizona invented a unique process of etching designs into shells. With the use of an acid derived from cactus, they produced an array of exquisitely decorated shells. Their discovery of this technique predated acid etching in Europe by at least three hundred years. At about the same time, the Indians of Mexico began to use the "lost wax" method

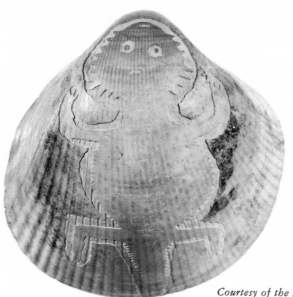

A horned lizard
etched with cactus acid
on a seashell.

Courtesy of the Arizona State Museum

to cast little copper bells, shaping models of the bells in wax and encasing the models in hard molds that were then filled with molten metal. The metal melted the wax and assumed its shape within the mold.

c. 1025 A.D.

The ancestors of the Navajo left their Athapaskan homeland in Alaska and western Canada and followed the trail of their Apache fellow Athapaskan southward into the agricultural lands of the Pueblos in Arizona and New Mexico.

c. 1150 A.D.

During the Classic Period of the Pueblo Culture in the southwestern part of North America, the Hopi Indians established the pueblo of Oraibi on the second of three mesas in northeastern Arizona. It is probably the oldest continuously occupied town in the United States.

c. 1100 A.D.

The golden age of the Pueblo people, the Classic Period of the Pueblo Culture, arose from three main influences—the Basketmakers collectively called Anasazi, "the ancient ones" once dominant in the vast plateau where Colorado, Utah, Arizona, and New Mexico meet; the Hohokam peoples of the desert to the south of the plateau, along the Gila and Salt rivers; and a third culture, the Mogollon, which once flowered in west-central New Mexico. The descendants of these cultures began drawing together in about 1050 to form large community centers; their most productive era lasted until the thirteenth century. The period is known for its architecture—compact masses of adjoining rooms piled four and five stories high. These complexes were built on mesa tops, across canyon floors, and in vast caverns that etched the sides of cliffs. Also typical of the Pueblo community were the ceremonial structures known as kivas, which were often built partially underground as an extension of the pit houses the ancestors of the Pueblo had built. Inside the kivas a rich ceremonial life took place, in conjunction with which symbolic murals were produced by exceptionally gifted Indian artists.

An original mural from Pottery Mound of a male with headdress and (right) a full-figure reproduction of the mural art.

1100–1300 A.D.

Between the tenth and twelfth centuries the Mimbres people, who evolved from the Mogollon Culture, developed a highly distinctive form of pottery. Some art historians believe this pottery was the invention of a single artist because of its consistent individuality. The pottery designs are both abstract in their symbols of clouds and other iconography, and uniquely narrative, depicting naturalistic figures of animals and people in what appear to be scenes that tell stories concerned with hunting, daily life, or rituals. The design, workmanship, and characteristic black paint applied to a white background represent an intriguing artistic achievement.

An example of Mimbres pottery.

Courtesy of the Museum of the American Indian, Heye Foundation

Often Mimbres pottery was deliberately broken in the center, or "killed," to release the power that the potter had invested in its creation before it was placed in the grave with the body of its owner.

c. 1200 A.D.

The Inca Indians of southern Peru began the construction of their empire, centered on the city of Cuzco, under the ruler Manco Capac.

c. 1224 A.D.

The Toltec civilization and its two hundred thirty-seven years of dominance in the Yucatán Peninsula came to an end when the Toltec inexplicably abandoned the great city of Chichén Itzá, which thereafter reverted to rule by the Maya-speaking Itzá.

Between 1263 and 1283 a joint rule was created in Chichén Itzá. Various states of the Yucatán region of Mexico took part in this central government, which was led by the Itzá. The Itzá also founded the city of Mayapán west of Chichén Itzá. Mayapán's ruling Itzá dynasty, the Cocom, eventually took control of the entire Yucatán. Mayapán was apparently the last stronghold of the Maya world.

The pyramid of Chichén Itzá.

c. 1265 A.D.

The Cascade Landslide on the Northwest Coast of North America occurred. Its debris reduced the drop at Celilo Falls on the Columbia River, allowing salmon to migrate upstream for the first time in over seven thousand years. Sahaptin-speaking peoples of the area again took up salmon fishing, which became central to their culture in post-Columbian times.

1276–99 A.D.

Severe drought devastated crops (this is shown by tree-ring dating) and caused the decline and abandonment of Indian cities in the southwestern part of North America. Mesa Verde cliff dwellings were abandoned after more than two hundred fifty years of occupation. At about the same time, the Anasazi abandoned the Four Corners area of the Southwest.

Cliff dwellings in Arizona.

This period of abandonment has been blamed on conditions other than drought. Commencing about 825 A.D., the ancestors of the Apache began to break away from northern Athapaskan groups and drift southward. In about 1025, the ancestors of the Navajo followed them. Their movement took them along the flanks of the Rockies into the Southwest. At first these Athapaskan probably just exploited the large unoccupied districts between the agricultural settlements of the Pueblo people; but as their numbers grew, they seem to have started to plunder the settlements themselves. Beginning in about 1200, there was a long period of warfare.

1325 A.D.

The Chapultepec Tenochca people founded Tenochtitlán, now Mexico City, on an island in Lake Texcoco. The Tenochca were called Mexica or Culhua-Mexica by the peoples of the Valley of Mexico; today they are generally known

The *Aztec Codex* drawing depicting the founding of Tenochtitlán.

as Aztec. Legend has it that they founded their capital as they had been instructed by their war god, Huitzilopochtli, at a place where they encountered an eagle with a serpent in its beak perched upon a cactus. (Today the eagle, serpent, and cactus are the Mexican national emblem.)

c. 1350–1600 A.D.

In the northeastern sector of what is now the United States, the Old Iroquois Culture developed gradually, producing bone needles, fishhooks, and implements used in weaving. The complex influence of the Mississippian Culture was little felt here. New methods of improving crops diffused from the Mississippian, but none of its opulent ceremonialism or mortuary rites reached the Old Iroquois people.

1440 A.D.

Montezuma I succeeded his uncle, Itzcóatl, as Aztec emperor. During his twenty-nine-year reign the empire expanded greatly. Montezuma pushed the frontier of the Aztec empire to the Gulf Coast and conquered the states of Puebla, Veracruz, Morelos, and Guerrero in Mexico.

c. 1441 A.D.

With the help of the Mexican Xiu people from the city of Uxmal, Mayapán's nobility killed all but one absent member of the ruling Cocom dynasty and overthrew the last centralized Maya government in the Yucatán. Mayapán was mysteriously abandoned after the uprising when the Xiu, the most awesome and militant group involved in the revolt, moved south to a city called

Maní. Subsequently the Maya world was devastated by a hurricane (in 1464), a plague (in 1480), and (in 1514) an epidemic of smallpox, which the conquistadors brought to America. Usually the disease preceded the conquistadors and greatly facilitated their military victories.

1469 A.D.

Axayácatl became the Aztec emperor, succeeding his grandfather, Montezuma I. During Axayácatl's twenty-year reign the famous Calendar, or Sun Stone, depicting a symbolic view of the Aztec cosmos, was carved. The stone was rediscovered in 1790 under what is now Mexico City's Plaza de la Constitución.

Courtesy of the Mexican National Tourist Council

The famous
Aztec Sun Stone.

C. 1470 A.D.

A series of droughts spanning forty years forced the abandonment of many High Plains villages. The concentration of Plains Indians in a smaller number of settlements called the Coalescent Tradition may have helped perpetuate the social "bands" of Plains Indians.

1487 A.D.

The Aztec and their allies the Texcocan dedicated a greatly remodeled and enlarged temple-pyramid to the god of war, Huitzilopochtli, and to the god of rain, Tlaloc, by sacrificing between twenty thousand and eighty thousand pris-

An Aztec depiction of the sacrifice of a human heart to the war god, Huitzilopochtli.

oners. Pictures created by Aztec artists who survived the invasion of Cortes depict this historic event: onlookers watch as a priest at the summit of the temple performs the sacrifice of a human heart to the war god, cutting it from the living victim's chest with an obsidian blade and holding it up to the sky while the body is thrown down the temple steps.

1492 A.D.

While the inhabitants of a small island in the Caribbean looked on in astonishment, a white man named Christopher Columbus, dressed in full armor and carrying the royal banner of Spain, waded ashore with his captains to claim the land for King Ferdinand and Queen Isabella of Spain. The inhabitants of the island, one of the Bahama group, called their home Guanahani, but Columbus chose to rename it San Salvador. "They took and gave all of whatever they had with good will," Columbus wrote, praising the Indians' friendliness and generosity. At the time there were more than nine million Indians in North America, speaking at least two hundred distinctive languages divided into seven major phyla, or groups of languages with the same general linguistic roots. The dialects of these languages, many of them mutually unintelligible, numbered into the several hundreds.

The very first people to whom Columbus gave the misnomer "Indians" (believing he had found a shortcut to the East Indies) were Arawak of the Greater Antilles Islands in the Caribbean.

c. 1500 A.D.

The Southern Cult reached its major flowering. Its ceremonial art of the Temple Mound Period represents some of the most accomplished Indian art produced in North America. A major region of the Southern Cult (near present-

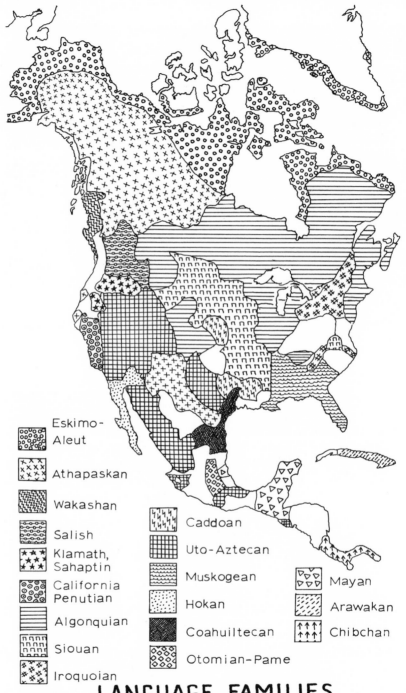

Eskimo-
Aleut

Athapaskan

Wakashan

Salish

Klamath,
Sahaptin

California
Penutian

Algonquian

Siouan

Iroquoian

Caddoan

Uto-Aztecan

Muskogean

Hokan

Coahuiltecan

Otomian-Pame

Mayan

Arawakan

Chibchan

LANGUAGE FAMILIES

Map drawn by Asa Battles

This warrior effigy pipe depicting a victor decapitating his victim is from Sprio Mound in Le Flore County, Oklahoma.

Courtesy of the Museum of the American Indian, Heye Foundation

day Natchez, Mississippi) was called the Plaquemine, and one of the chiefdoms of the Plaquemine, the Natchez, was one of the most bizarre social groups in the Americas.

There were two classes in Natchez society—nobles and commoners. The nobles called the commoners "stinkards." The nobles, on the other hand, were called "suns," "nobles," or "honoreds," depending on their status. The Great Sun was at the peak of the Natchez social system.

All members of the Natchez nobility were required to marry stinkards. Children whose fathers were commoners inherited the ranks of their mothers, while children whose mothers were commoners were born to the next rank below that of their fathers. It was a very complex system made even more complicated by an elaborate scheme of etiquette.

The power of the Great Sun was unlimited. His father was necessarily a commoner, and the Great Sun therefore inherited his office from his mother, called the White Woman, who in turn was the eldest sister of the previous Great Sun. Normally the Great Sun passed his office to his sister's son when he died. At the time of his death, the wives and retainers of the Great Sun were marked for sacrifice or ritual suicide. The Great Sun's body and that of his primary wife were borne on a litter to the temple along a path covered with the bodies of strangled infants. Those who were to accompany them in death took potions of tobacco that caused them to lose consciousness, and they were ritualistically strangled by their closest relatives. Then all were buried or cremated, and the house of the Great Sun was burned to the ground. These were people who had adopted the most rigid political and religious concepts of Mexican civilization and perpetuated them to the point of fanaticism.

1503 A.D.

Montezuma II speaks to his council—a picture by an Aztec artist.

Montezuma II, the most famous Aztec emperor (surnamed Xocoyotzin, "the Younger"), was crowned in Tenochtitlán. He was the nephew of Ahuízotl, eighth leader of the Aztec, and the son of the emperor who succeeded Montezuma I, Axayácatl. Montezuma II was an able ruler who greatly enlarged his empire, added stature to Tenochtitlán (Mexico City), and put down numerous rebellious peoples, who completely surrounded the Aztec domain. These enemies eventually allied themselves with the Spanish invaders in order to crush their Aztec overlords, only to find themselves destroyed in turn by the Spanish once they had helped to overthrow the Aztec empire.

1507 A.D.

The last Aztec New Fire Ceremony was celebrated, signifying the end of one fifty-two-year cycle and the beginning of another. This was a major religious event among a people for whom astronomy and time cycles were of the utmost importance. Aztec priests kindled the new flame—which ritualistically brought in the new fifty-two-year cycle—in the open chest of a sacrificial victim, and then runners carried the flame to all parts of the empire. It was the will of the gods that permitted the new cycle to begin, and the Aztec spent the last day of the old cycle fasting and praying. At sunset their priests mounted the extinct volcano, Huixachtecatl (now Cerro de la Estrella), southeast of

Mexico City, and there they awaited the gods' signal of consent for their continued existence—the movement of a star to a specified position in the heavens. When the signal was given in 1507 it marked the beginning of the last time cycle of the Aztec world.

1507–19 A.D.

It was the belief of the Aztec that their god of air, a white-skinned and bearded diety named Quetzalcóatl, the Feathered Serpent, would return from the sea at this time. Furthermore, the period just before the beginning of the new fifty-two-year cycle had been a time of great anxiety for the Aztec. Thus, a series of events that occurred at this time greatly frightened Montezuma II and his people: a devastating flood, without apparent cause, in the capital; a mysterious fire that could not be extinguished in the great temple; three comets in the night sky; and a strange, pyramid-shaped light rising from the horizon and

In these works from the *Florentine Codex,* ancient Aztec artists depict the ominous series of events that occurred just before white men were seen arriving on the shores of the Aztec Empire.

terrifying the Aztec. Finally—when Montezuma's sages had advised him that the downfall of the Aztec empire was at hand—the emperor received the incredible news that white men with beards had been seen on the coast of Yucatán.

1513 A.D.

Calusa Indians in eighty war canoes drove the ships of the Spanish explorer Juan Ponce de León from the western coast of Florida. Ponce de León was the first European known to have had extensive contact with North American Indians. In 1521, he died in what is now Havana, Cuba, after escaping by sea from the Florida Indians who had fatally wounded him.

1519 A.D.

On April 21 in the year Aztec sages prophesied the return of Quetzalcóatl, the tall, dark-haired, white-skinned, bearded god of the winds, the Spanish conquistador Hernando Cortes, perfectly fitting the god's description, landed near the Totonac town of Quiahuiztlán (the site of modern Veracruz, Mexico) with one hundred sailors, five hundred eight soldiers, sixteen horses, and fourteen cannons. In the Aztec capital, the emperor Montezuma II silenced his advisors and decided to appease the invaders by sending rich gifts—at the same time ordering the Spanish not to approach his capital, Tenochtitlán. Cortes, meanwhile, undertook a bizarre military tactic—he ordered that his ships be burned to prevent the flight of his men. Had Montezuma attacked rather than attempting to appease the small Spanish band, he might easily have driven the six hundred eight strangers into the sea. Presumably Montezuma's decision to be peaceable was based on Cortes' curious resemblance to the legendary Quetzalcóatl.

1519 A.D.

Cortes and Montezuma II speak through the woman interpreter, Malintzin.

On November 8, emperor Montezuma II met Hernando Cortes at the edge of the Aztec capital of Tenochtitlán and passively led the Spanish invaders and their Tlaxcalan Indian allies (long enemies of the Aztec) into the city. The Aztec had made no substantial efforts to halt the three-month-long Spanish march from Quiahuiztlán on the Gulf Coast. A week later, Montezuma was made a prisoner by the Spanish, who then commenced to plunder the Aztec riches. In the famous *Florentine Codex* are found pictures created by Mexican Indians shortly after their subjugation; these depict, among other events, the meeting of Cortes and Montezuma with Malintzin, or Doña Marina. Malintzin, a woman given to Cortes as a gift by the Aztec, acted as interpreter between the two.

1520 A.D.

Montezuma II, held prisoner by the Spanish, was deposed by the Aztec royal council and replaced by his brother, Cuitláhuac. A short time later, on June 30, Montezuma died—possibly of wounds inflicted by his Aztec subjects on June 29 while he was addressing them in an attempt to convince them not to resist conquest by the Spaniards. The Aztec believed, however, that Montezuma was strangled by the Spaniards, and they might have been right.

1521 A.D.

Despite fierce resistance, Tenochtitlán, the Aztec capital, was taken on August 13 by the small Spanish contingent and a vast army of Indians who were long-standing enemies of the Aztec. The capital was under siege for ninety days, with food and fresh water supplies cut off. After the defeat, the Spaniards totally destroyed the city and began building Mexico City on the ruins.

The Spaniards march on Tenochtitlán and (right) burn the capital after defeating the Aztec.

1523–24 A.D.

Giovanni da Verrazano, the Florentine navigator, looking for a route to the Pacific Ocean, explored the Atlantic coast by ship from the area of South Carolina as far north as Nova Scotia. He encountered Wampanoag, Narragansett, and Delaware Indians in the Delaware and Chesapeake bay districts of the east coast of North America. The Indians were largely cautious of the explorer and his party, possibly having heard stories of slave raids being conducted by Europeans along the North Atlantic coast.

1528–36 A.D.

Pánfilio de Narváez, Alvar Nuñez Cabeza de Vaca, and four hundred men, eighty horses, and five ships set out to colonize Florida. Their ships were wrecked and the party was decimated. At least four men survived: Cabeza de Vaca, Esteban the Moor, Andrés Dorantes, and Alonzo del Castillo. These men eventually arrived in Culiacan, Sinaloa, in western Mexico, having walked there from the east coast of Texas and having had contacts and confrontations with many Indian tribes in the Southwest en route. Though Spanish history books make these men out to be heroes, Indians have accused the party of exploitation and aggression, and Esteban, in particular, is looked upon by Pueblo Indians as a thief and a rapist.

1532 A.D.

On November 16, Atahuallpa, the emperor of the great Inca civilization of Peru, held a meeting with Francisco Pizarro, the Spanish conquistador, at Cajamarca. Though the Spanish were greatly outnumbered, they managed to seize Atahuallpa during the "peace talks" and make him a prisoner. The ransom demanded for the Inca ruler was a room filled with gold and silver treasure.

1533 A.D.

The Inca ruler, Atahuallpa, was executed on August 29 by his Spanish captors by order of Francisco Pizarro, who is often called the most ruthless of the Spanish conquistadors. On November 15, the Spanish forced their way into the Inca capital of Cuzco, which they took in the name of Spain.

Courtesy of Perutour, Inc.

A herd of llama before the ancient stone walls of Cuzco.

1539–43 A.D.

Hernando de Soto formally took possession of Florida. He then traveled through what is now the southeastern United States—Georgia, Alabama, Louisiana, Mississippi, and parts of Arkansas—in search of Indian wealth he hoped might be comparable in richness to the plunder his countrymen had gotten in Mexico and Peru. His expedition was a disaster for the Indian tribes he confronted; they were left with a terrible impression of white men. De Soto eventually died on the banks of the Mississippi River in 1541, and Luis de Moscoso took over as leader of the expedition. Moscoso and the three hundred eleven surviving Florida colonists (there had originally been six hundred) fled by ship to Panuco, Mexico, where they arrived in 1543. De Soto and his colonists had made permanent enemies for the white man of the Creek, Hitchiti, Chickasaw, Chakchiuma, Choctaw, Tunica, Yuchi, Cherokee, and Alibamu tribes.

Creek-Seminole artist Jerome Tiger depicts "The Intruders." This painting shows Seminole warriors watching the approach of the Spanish invaders.

1540–42 A.D.

Francisco Vásquez de Coronado, with three hundred Spanish soldiers and about a thousand Indians, explored the southwestern part of North America in a vain search for the fabled Seven Cities of Cibola, a metropolis reportedly made of gold. Instead of finding golden cities Coronado found seven mud-and-brick pueblos of the Zuñi Indians. His expedition also encountered Hopi, Lipan, Jicarilla, Mescalero, and other Indian tribes before finally reaching the fabled land of Quivira (which became Kansas) and turning back empty-handed. Quivira was inhabited by Wichita Indians who did not know what gold was.

1542 A.D.

Juan Cabrillo, a Spanish explorer, landed at San Diego, California, and met Indians who indicated that they were aware of Coronado's cruelties during his expeditions in the Southwest. Though the Indians did not trust Cabrillo, he managed to explore the coast as far north as Point Reyes.

1564–65 A.D.

The French Huguenots under René de Laudonniere established a relatively friendly relationship with the Indians near the mouth of St. John's River in Florida, and the French colonized the area until the Spanish drove them out. Among the Huguenots was the artist Jacques Le Moyne, whose paintings of Indians (which were subsequently engraved in Europe) were the first pictures by a white man of North American Indians.

1565 A.D.

After enormous resistance from the Indians of the area, the Spanish established St. Augustine, Florida; it was to be the first successful and permanent European colony in North America. This was the beginning of the major invasion of North America by the white man.

c. 1570 A.D.

The Iroquois Five-Nation Confederacy, according to tradition, was founded at about this time by Dekanawida, a Huron Indian prophet and statesman, and his Mohawk disciple Hiawatha (*not* the Hiawatha of Longfellow's poem). To form this coalition it was necessary for the Cayuga, Mohawk, Oneida, Onondaga, and Seneca tribes to put aside their feuds. The resulting Iroquois League (as it was called) became the most powerful of all the North American Indian confederacies; it numbered over sixteen thousand people in 1677 and could be a strong ally or foe in the various wars between white men that eventually preoccupied the French, English, and Americans in their efforts to gain dominance in North America.

An Indian depiction of Atotarho, the Medusa-headed Onondaga chief whose conversion to the Great Peace marked the foundation of the Iroquois League.

1579 A.D.

Sir Francis Drake explored the coast of California by ship, visiting the Miwok Indians north of San Francisco Bay and other tribes, and establishing himself as one of the most detested of European invaders.

1585–86 A.D.

The first English colony in North America was established on Roanoke Island, North Carolina. Despite the financial backing of Sir Walter Raleigh, the colony lasted for less than a year, so unadept at survival in the food-rich American environment were the first colonists.

1587–90 A.D.

Raleigh's second attempt to establish a colony at Roanoke ended in failure—and with the mysterious disappearance of the entire colony. According to Indians of the area, the colonists abandoned their failing settlement and were peacefully assimilated into various Indian villages. John White, the governor of Roanoke, sailed back to England before the disappearance of the colony, taking with him the now famous paintings and drawings of native North Americans that he had produced at Roanoke.

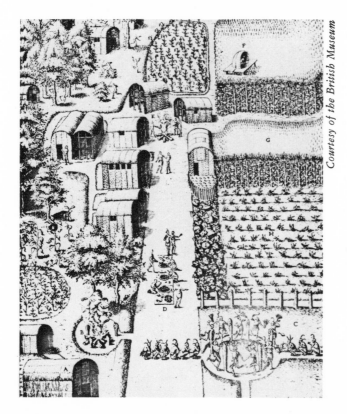

Courtesy of the British Museum

John White's drawing of the town of Secotan—one of the most complete representations of the daily life of sixteenth-century Indians of the Atlantic seaboard.

1598 A.D.

Juan de Oñate succeeded in founding the first permanent Spanish colony in the American Southwest, San Gabriel del Yunque, in northern New Mexico. It is known today as San Juan Indian Pueblo.

1598 A.D.

The Tewa Indians of the pueblo called Yugeuingge voluntarily gave up their town on the Rio Grande to Spanish colonists under Juan de Oñate, who had become governor of Spanish New Mexico. The Indians moved across the river, where they lived with the Tewa Indians of San Juan Pueblo, who welcomed them.

1598–99 A.D.

The Indians of Acoma Pueblo, a town perched on a three-hundred-fifty-foot rock mesa in New Mexico, attacked a group of thirty visiting Spaniards in December, 1598. A year later the Spanish sent a retaliatory force that, in a three-day battle, killed about fifteen hundred Indians and forced the surviving fifteen hundred inhabitants of Acoma to submit to Spanish rule.

c. 1600 A.D.

The use of wool was introduced in the Southwest when Indians began raising sheep (which had been brought to America by the Spaniards). At about the same time, the Indians of the Southwest began weaving with the "true loom." Indians in other areas made textiles by finger-weaving without a loom.

A chief's blanket crafted by the Navajo.

1600 A.D.

Henry Hudson, the British navigator, went in search of a "northwest passage" in behalf of the Dutch. He explored the river that now bears his name, seeking a way from the Atlantic to the Pacific and thence to India.

c. 1600–65 A.D.

The Mississippian Culture of the southern sector of the Eastern Woodlands collapsed under the pressure of progressive European invasion and the impact of disease. Some of the people migrated to the Great Plains, where they adopted the life-style of the mounted nomads of the region, who were managing to hold their own against the pioneers and cavalry.

c. 1600–75 A.D.

The Spanish horse—which was already integrated into the cultures of the desert area of the American West—was introduced into the Great Plains, and greatly changed the lives of the people there. The horse made the Plains Indians highly mobile as hunters and warriors and therefore their diet improved, they were better able to exploit the natural resources of their homeland, and they became effective in their battle against the white invaders.

Courtesy of the Roberts Museum, Pierre, South Dakota

A Dakota wooden effigy horse.

c. 1600–1700 A.D.

Indians of what is now western Nebraska, living in circular earthen lodges and belonging to what is called the Dismal River Culture, lived primarily by hunting buffalo, deer, beaver, elk, and turtles. By this date dogs had long been domesticated locally, and may sometimes have been used as food. Agriculture was not highly developed, but some corn and squash were probably grown.

1607 A.D.

Powhatan Indians captured a group of explorers from the newly established Virginia colony of Jamestown as they were making their way up the Chicahominy River in December. The colonists were led by the English soldier Captain John Smith. According to Smith's story, he was released by the Indians at the request of the Powhatan chief's daughter, Pocahontas—an improbable tale that nevertheless became the basis of one of early America's sentimental romances.

Powhatan waiting to receive the English prisoner John Smith.

Courtesy of the New York Public Library

c. 1608 A.D.

Powhatan, chief of the Powhatan Indian Confederacy of about thirty tribes that inhabited the territory surrounding the Jamestown colony in Virginia, was crowned king by Captain John Smith, with complete royal regalia sent from England. The pomp did not impress Powhatan for long; he soon lost enthusiasm for the English, and only the kidnapping of his daughter, Pocahontas, and her subsequent marriage to John Rolfe, an Englishman, dissuaded him from devastating the Virginia colony.

1609 A.D.

Powhatan spoke to Captain John Smith, saying, "Why should you take by force that from us which you can have by love? Why should you destroy us, who have provided you with food? What can you get by war? We can hide our provisions, and fly into the woods; and then you must consequently famish by wronging your friends. What is the cause of your jealousy? You see us unarmed, and willing to supply your wants, if you will come in a friendly manner, and not with swords and guns, as to invade an enemy. I am not so simple as not to know it is better to eat good meat, lie well, and sleep quietly with my women and children; to laugh and be merry with the English; and, being their friend, to have copper, hatchets, and whatever else I want, than to fly from all, to lie cold in the woods, to feed upon acorns, roots, and such trash, and to be so hunted that I cannot rest, eat, or sleep."

1609 A.D.

The title page of Henry Hudson's journal, published in 1663.

Two canoes full of Manhattan Indians attacked the *Half Moon,* the ship of the explorer Henry Hudson, as it sailed down the Hudson River in New York State. Later he encountered other Indians living in circular bark lodges who greeted him. Hudson reported, "The natives were good people, for when they saw I would not remain with them, they supposed I was afraid of their bows and arrows, and taking the arrows they broke them into pieces and threw them into the fire."

1621 A.D.

On March 22, Massassoit, chief of the Wampanoag Indians, a principal tribe of New England, signed the first treaty ever made with Europeans—the Pilgrims of Plymouth—freely granting them land.

1623 A.D.

On May 6, the Manhattan Indians of the Wappinger Indian Confederacy in eastern North America sold the island of Manhattan to Peter Minuit, the Dutch governor of New Amsterdam (now New York). The Indians had used the island only for hunting and fishing, since they had found its climate too extreme for comfortable living. The Dutch paid sixty guilders (or twenty-four American dollars) in red cloth, beads, buttons, and other items for Manhattan.

The first known picture of New Amsterdam, c. 1626.

1637 A.D.

The Pequot War was fought in Massachusetts. It was caused by the death of a white trader who was killed by Pequot Indians who claimed he had mistreated them. Captain John Mason and his soldiers (with the help of Mohegan Indians) killed more than five hundred men, women, and children in a surprise attack on the Pequot village near the Mystic River. Governor Bradford of Plymouth Colony wrote, "It was a fearful sight to see them frying in the fire and the streams of blood quenching the same, and horrible was the stink and stench thereof. But the victory seemed a sweet sacrifice and they gave praise thereof to God."

1641 A.D.

Willem Kleft, governor of New Netherlands, offered a bounty of ten to twelve guilders (four to five dollars) for Raritan Indian heads. The Raritan had killed four Staten Island farmers.

1661 A.D.

The first Bible published in North America was John Eliot's translation into the Algonquian language.

1661 A.D.

In an effort to suppress Indian religious ceremonies among the Pueblo Indians of New Mexico, the Spanish authorities raided their sacred kivas (ceremonial

A Hopi kachina.

houses) and destroyed sixteen hundred kachina masks that represented the powers central to Pueblo religion.

c. 1670 A.D.

The ten thousand Indians of New England were by this time greatly outnumbered by the seventy-five thousand white settlers. Not only had the Indians suffered losses through war and disease, but their land holdings had also been reduced by nearly half.

c. 1675 A.D.

In the eastern parts of America, Indians began to use European glass beads (called "trade beads" because they were originally used as money when whites bartered with Indians) to decorate apparel. Gradually beads replaced the porcupine quillwork that had been used to decorate hide clothing, moccasins, headbands, and pipe bags.

A bag decorated with beadwork.

1675–78 A.D.

Most of the tribes of New England were allied in a war against the British, called "King Philip's War" after a Wampanoag leader whose name was really Metacom. After many battles the surrender of the Indians took place on

August 28, 1676. ("King Philip" himself was killed on August 12, after which his wife and son were sold into slavery in the West Indies.) The defeat broke the power of the Algonquian Indians in New England, but victory cost the British one sixth of their male population in the region (six hundred men).

1680 A.D.

Led by a Tewa Indian medicine man named Popé, the Pueblo people banded together in a rare instance of military cooperation between the villages and drove the Spanish out of their lands. The revolt took place on August 10; about four hundred colonists were killed, and the remaining three thousand were forced to flee southward into Mexico. With the Spanish ejected, the Indians burned and destroyed all traces of Christian culture, and ritually used suds from the yucca plant to cleanse all the Indians who had been baptized.

A purification rite.

1692–94 A.D.

The Spaniards succeeded in their attempt to reconquer the Indians of New Mexico, whose will to fight was greatly weakened by famine, internal dissension that destroyed their unity, drought, and the attacks of marauding bands of Apache from the north.

1689–97 A.D.

King William's War, the first of four wars for European control of the eastern region of North America, was fought. In the struggle, the Indians were used by both the British and the French, and in turn played the European powers off against each other. The tribes recognized too late that they were exterminating one another and that the white settlers were the only ones making any gains from the conflicts.

1700 A.D.

In a gesture of outrage and defiance of Spanish rule, the Hopi Indians attacked and destroyed one of their own towns, Awatobi, Arizona, killing or capturing all the Indian inhabitants who had fallen under Christian missionary influence.

1702–13 A.D.

The British and French engaged in a confrontation called "Queen Anne's War" in the southeastern part of North America. This struggle eventually involved numerous eastern Indian tribes. One at a time, the British defeated the Indian allies of the French—the Alabama, Chickasaw, Creek, and Yazoo Indians.

After the French were defeated they conceded Britain's sovereignty over the Iroquois tribes of the Northeast.

1720 A.D.

Spaniards also battled the French. In 1720 in the region of what is now Nebraska, the French and their Pawnee and Oto Indian allies won a victory over Spanish soldiers and their Pueblo Indian allies. The French commander was Don Pedro de Villasur. A painting of this battle by a Spanish-trained Indian artist was sent by a priest to his brother in Switzerland; there this now famous depiction of the battle was found by the Swiss scholar Gottfried Hotz.

Courtesy of Gottfried Hotz

The French commander Don Pedro de Villasur and his Indian allies defeat the Spanish and their Indian allies.

1722 A.D.

The Tuscarora Indians were officially recognized as members of the Iroquois Confederacy, and the confederacy became known as the Six Nations. The Tuscarora had been living among the Iroquois in northeastern North America since their escape from North Carolina in about 1713.

1751 A.D.

Benjamin Franklin, attempting to promote colonial union and cooperation, cited the Iroquois Six-Nation Confederacy as a possible model for the colonies to emulate. Aspects of the structure of the confederacy were incorporated into the Constitution and laws of the United States of America when it became a nation.

1754–63 A.D.

The French and Indian War, fought by the British and their Indian allies against the French and their Indian allies, resulted in British domination of Canada. The Iroquois Six-Nation Confederacy allied itself with the British, while many of the Algonquian tribes sided with the French. The defeat of the French meant British reprisals against the Algonquian peoples.

1755 A.D.

The Albany Board of Indian Commissioners was stripped of its power and William Johnson became the English Superintendent of Indian Affairs for the Northern Department of North America. Edmond Atkins was named to a similar post in the South in 1756. Atkins advocated liquor control among Indian traders. He recommended that traders should "incur a penalty for any Indian getting Drunk with such Liquor, that being the only cause of almost every mischief they do; and the greatest Destruction of their Numbers."

1758 A.D.

The first Indian reservation in North America was established by the New Jersey colonial assembly. The three-thousand-acre tract in Burlington County, called Edge Pillock, was settled by about one hundred Indians, most of them from the Unami tribe.

1760 A.D.

By this time the horse had become a vital and established part of the culture of the Cheyenne and other Indian tribes of the North American plains. The mastery of the breeding and riding of this animal permitted the Indians to

Chasing horses, as depicted by Howling Wolf.

excel as nomadic hunters of buffalo and other wild game in the Great Plains area.

1763 A.D.

King George III of England issued a royal proclamation defining Indian country as "any lands beyond the heads or sources of any of the rivers which fall into the Atlantic Ocean from the West or Northwest," thus granting Indians the lands west of the Appalachian Mountains. The proclamation also prohibited British subjects from transacting private business involving Indian lands, and under its terms Indian tribes were regarded as sovereign entities on a par with the British. The proclamation was highly unpopular with the American colonists, who claimed that it interfered with their affairs. The British effort to enforce the proclamation was one of the major causes for the ensuing Revolutionary War between the colonists and Great Britain.

1764 A.D.

A bounty was offered by the Pennsylvania Assembly for the scalp of every enemy Indian above ten years old. The scalping of whites by Indians was limited until the bounty system was established by the colonists.

1767–68 A.D.

The effective and compassionate Jesuit missionaries were expelled by King Charles III of Spain from New Spain, which included the American Southwest. Without their leadership, the missions built to convert Indians deteriorated, and by 1820 few Christian centers remained among the tribes.

Courtesy of the Museum of the American Indian, Heye Foundation

The church, by Bear's Heart.

1773 A.D.

Mexican Indians of the Chiapas region came upon the ruins of the ancient Maya city of Palenque and informed a local priest of their discovery. The city had been entirely forgotten by the Indians of the region. Charles III of Spain sent a royal commission to investigate and to preserve artifacts.

The Temple of the Inscriptions, Palenque.

Photograph by the author

1775 A.D.

On July 12, the American Continental Congress appropriated the sum of five hundred dollars for the education of Indian youth at Dartmouth College in New Hampshire. Dartmouth College began its history in Lebanon, Connecticut, as Moor's Indian Charity School, which was founded in 1750. In 1769 the school moved to Hanover, New Hampshire, and was eventually chartered as Dartmouth College.

1776 A.D.

The rebels of the American Revolution cited as one of the offenses committed by England's King George III the arousing of antagonism between Indians and colonists. The American Declaration of Independence, adopted on July 4, stated, "He has excited domestic insurrections amongst us, and has endeavoured to bring on the inhabitants of our frontiers, the merciless Indian Savages, whose known rule of warfare, is an undistinguished destruction, of all ages, sexes and conditions." The United States of America was born.

1778 A.D.

The first treaty negotiated between the newly founded United States and an Indian tribe was signed by the Delaware Indians and the Americans on September 17. In it, the Delaware were offered the prospect of statehood.

1779 A.D.

The Iroquois Confederacy tribes aided the British in western Pennsylvania and New York during the American War of Independence. Therefore, General George Washington sent General John Sullivan and about four thousand soldiers to march against the Iroquois. In retaliation for the Iroquois' alliance with the British, General Sullivan left forty Indian towns a smoking waste, and his troops burned one hundred sixty thousand bushels of corn and other crops. The power of the Iroquois Confederacy was broken, and the Iroquois never recovered from this attack.

c. 1780 A.D.

A decorative craft called ribbonwork came into use among the southern tribes of the Great Lakes area and also developed, a bit later, among the Oto, Osage, and Seminole. Clothing was decorated with ribbon appliqués—colored ribbons

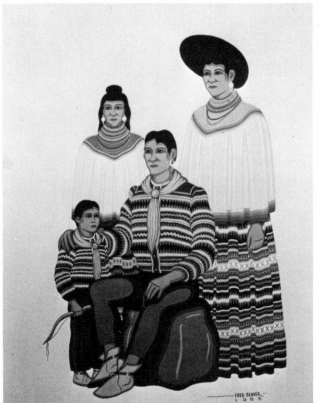

Courtesy of the Philbrook Art Center, Tulsa

"Seminole Family,"
by Fred Beaver.

of silk and satin cut into elaborate designs and sewn on the garments. Though the materials were European (they were acquired in trade), the method and style of the craft were distinctly Indian.

1787 A.D.

The American states adopted a Constitution that noted that the federal government alone had the power to "regulate commerce with foreign nations, and among the several states, and with the Indian tribes, within the limits of any state, not subject to the laws thereof." Combined with the government's power to negotiate treaties and to enact other laws, the clause provided the basis of subsequent federal legislation and judicial decisions involving Indians.

1790–99 A.D.

Four Trade and Intercourse acts concerning Indians became federal law. They required public treaty for the purchase of Indian lands; set out the boundaries of Indian country; established government trading houses (the "factory system," as it was called); and provided for the appointment by the President of Indian agents to conduct affairs with Indians. Enforcement of laws regarding Indians was placed in the hands of an informal "Indian department" with the War Department.

1791 A.D.

The Miami Indian chief Little Turtle, leading a combined force of Miami, Delaware, Shawnee, Chippewa, Potawatomi, and Ottawa Indians, inflicted the worst defeat the United States suffered in the history of its wars with Indians.

General Arthur St. Clair lost six hundred thirty men out of a total of fourteen hundred, and more than three hundred men were wounded. The battle was fought near the Miami River in Ohio.

1799 A.D.

Handsome Lake, a Seneca chief, had visions that led him to form the Code of Handsome Lake and subsequently to found a new Indian religion. The Long House Religion is widely practiced today among Iroquois Indians of northern New York and southeastern Canada.

"The Code of Handsome Lake," by Ernest Smith.

Courtesy of American Indian Treasures, Inc., Guilderland, New York

c. 1800 A.D.

Silver was never worked extensively by the pre-Columbian tribes of North America, but by 1800 the Iroquois and other northeastern tribes were making their own silver ornaments. The craft spread quickly to the Great Lakes and west to the Plains and Prairie peoples, and eventually influenced the development of silverwork among the Navajo.

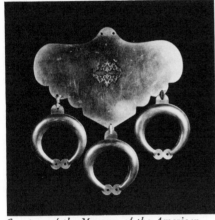

A breast ornament of German silver made by a Kiowa Indian craftsman of Oklahoma.

Courtesy of the Museum of the American Indian, Heye Foundation

1802 A.D.

A federal law was passed controlling the vending of liquor to Indians; Congress conferred the power to enforce this law on the President.

1802 A.D.

Congress appropriated a sum of money, not to exceed fifteen thousand dollars a year, "to promote civilization among the aborigines."

1805 A.D.

Carrying her infant, Sacajawea, a young Lemhi Shoshone Indian woman, guided the Lewis and Clark expedition up the Missouri River and through the Rocky Mountains into the Great Plains.

1812 A.D.

The Russians established Fort Ross among the Pomo Indians in northwestern California despite heavy Indian resistance.

1813 A.D.

Tecumseh, a Shawnee leader and organizer of a large Indian confederacy, was killed leading an Indian army against Americans near Chatham, Ontario. Tecumseh had allied his forces with the British in the War of 1812 in an attempt to stop the westward flood of American settlers, whom he detested. "The way," Tecumseh proclaimed, "the only way to stop this evil is for the red men to unite in claiming a common and equal right in the land, as it was at first, and should be now—for it was never divided, but belongs to all. No tribe has the right to sell, even to each other, much less to strangers. . . . *Sell a country? Why not sell the air, the great sea, as well as the earth?* Did not the Great Power make them all for the use of his children? How can we have confidence in the white people? When their Jesus Christ came upon the earth they killed him and nailed him to the cross. They thought he was dead, and they were mistaken. [The white people] have Shakers among them and they laugh and make light of [the Shakers'] form of worship. Everything I have told you is the truth."

1821 A.D.

A Cherokee Indian named Sequoyah, after working for twelve years, completed his famous alphabet for the Cherokee language. There had been no written languages among North American Indians prior to Sequoyah's invention of Cherokee syllabary, which was based on a combination of the Roman alphabet and other symbols. The creation of a written form of the Cherokee language (and its eventual use to print a weekly newspaper, *The Cherokee Phoenix,* and parts of the Bible) was an effort by the Cherokee to prove to whites that Indians could be "civilized." The effort, however, did not prevent the Cherokee from being removed from their native lands in the southeast to Indian Territory (Oklahoma) despite a long, raging legal battle to resist removal.

The Cherokee alphabet invented by Sequoyah made a Cherokee newspaper possible.

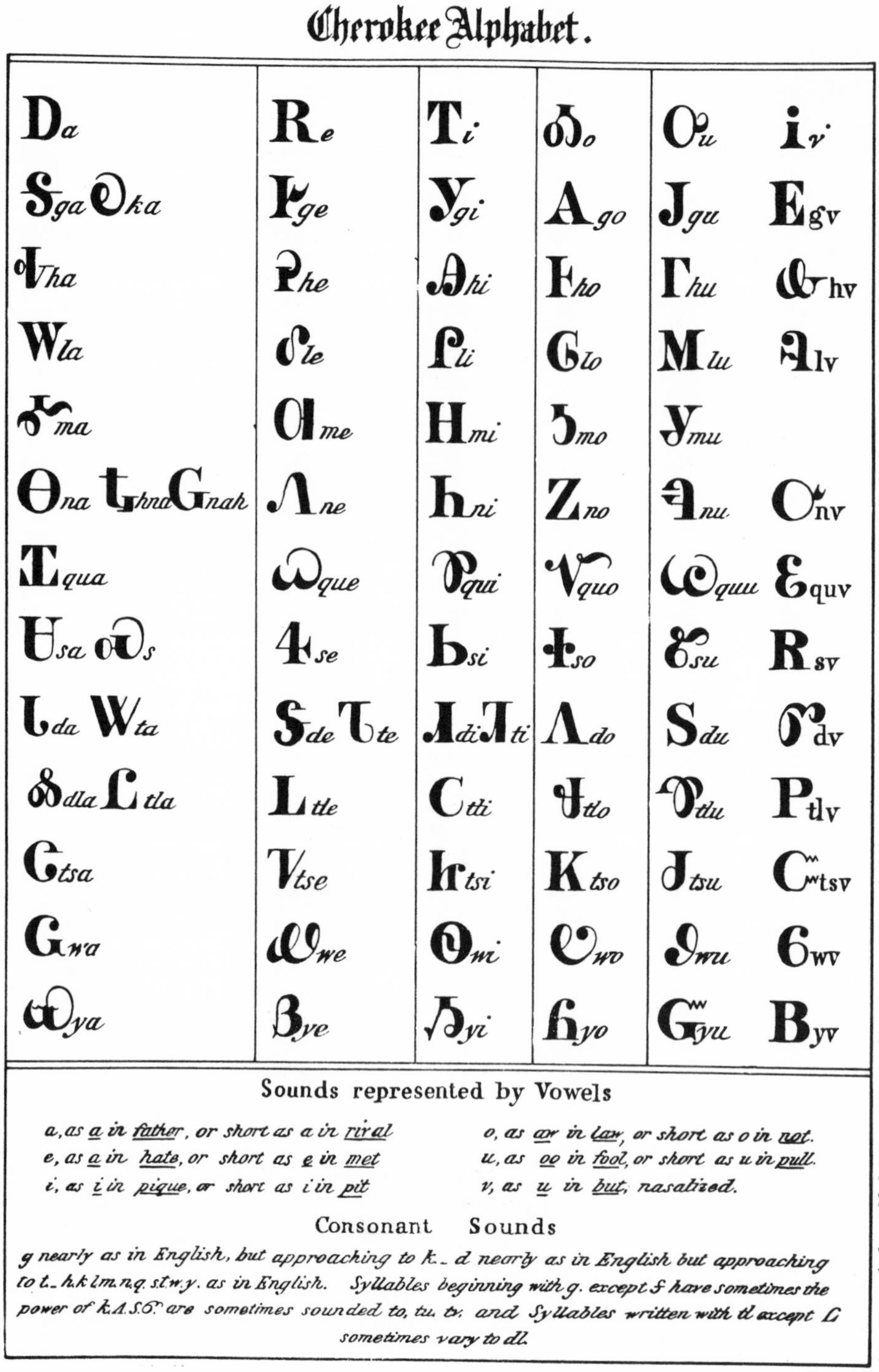

Cherokee Alphabet.

D a	R e	T i	Ꮿ o	O u	i v
S ga Ꭴ ka	Ꭶ ge	Ꮿ gi	A go	J gu	E gv
Ꮚ ha	Ꮖ he	Ꮙ hi	Ꮚ ho	Ꮇ hu	Ꮾ hv
W la	Ꮊ le	Ꮕ li	G lo	M lu	� lv
Ꮉ ma	Ꭴ me	H mi	Ꮽ mo	Ꮿ mu	
Ꮎ na Ꮏ hna Ꮐ nah	Λ ne	Ꮧ ni	Z no	Ꮔ nu	Ꮕ nv
Ꮖ qua	Ꮗ que	Ꮙ qui	Ꮚ quo	Ꮙ quu	Ꮛ quv
Ꮜ sa Ꮝ s	4 se	Ꮟ si	Ꮠ so	Ꮢ su	R sv
Ꮣ da Ꮤ ta	Ꮥ de Ꮦ te	Ꮧ di Ꮨ ti	Λ do	S du	Ꮬ dv
Ꮝ dla Ꮮ tla	L tle	C tli	Ꮰ tlo	Ꮱ tlu	P tlv
Ꮳ tsa	Ꮴ tse	Ꮵ tsi	K tso	J tsu	C tsv
Ꮹ wa	Ꮺ we	Ꮻ wi	Ꮼ wo	Ꮽ wu	6 wv
Ꮿ ya	Ᏸ ye	Ᏹ yi	Ᏺ yo	G yu	B yv

Sounds represented by Vowels

a, as _a_ in _father_, or short as a in _rival_

e, as _a_ in _hate_, or short as _e_ in _met_

i, as _i_ in _pique_, or short as i in _pit_

o, as _aw_ in _law_, or short as o in _not_.

u, as _oo_ in _fool_, or short as u in _pull_.

v, as _u_ in _but_, nasalized.

Consonant Sounds

g nearly as in English, but approaching to k. d nearly as in English but approaching to t. h.k.l.m.n.q. s.t.w.y. as in English. Syllables beginning with g. except Ꮝ have sometimes the power of k.Ꭺ.Ꮝ.Ꮯ. are sometimes sounded to, tu, tv. and Syllables written with tl except Ꮣ sometimes vary to dl.

Sequoyah's Cherokee syllabary.

1824 A.D.

The Bureau of Indian Affairs was formally organized within the War Department.

1830 A.D.

An Indian Removal Bill passed Congress by a small margin of votes, permitting the removal of Indians from the eastern United States to lands west of the Mississippi River, provided the Indians gave their consent. Often Indians who did not officially represent the majority of their people were urged to sign treaties approving removal. The Cherokee contested the law in the courts.

1832 A.D.

In the case of Samuel A. Worcester vs. the State of Georgia (which actually involved the Cherokee Indians and their removal), the United States Supreme Court decided in favor of the Cherokee, specifying that states do not have jurisdiction over Indian lands and affairs.

1834 A.D.

The U.S. Department of Indian Affairs was created by Congress, resulting in a reorganization of the offices that had previously dealt with Indian affairs.

1835–38 A.D.

Despite a Supreme Court ruling, removal of the Cherokee Indians of Georgia to lands west of the Mississippi River was carried out by seven thousand federal troops under General Winfield Scott. A small group of Cherokee agreed to removal in 1835, and this was excuse enough for the white men to move them all out. Beginning in May, 1838, the Indians were forcibly rounded up. In October, 1838, the Indians began their trek westward under military escort; the wintery route they followed has become known as "The Trail of Tears." Of the seventeen thousand Cherokee emigrants, more than four thousand perished because of the extreme hardships of the journey and the bitter winter weather. The survivors reached northeastern Oklahoma late in March, 1839. All five "civilized tribes" (the Cherokee, Seminole, Creek, Choctaw, and Chickasaw) were eventually relocated in Oklahoma. The people of all five tribes suffered great hardships while they were being removed.

Creek-Seminole artist Jerome Tiger depicts "The Trail of Tears."

Courtesy of Mrs. Peggy Tiger

1835–42 A.D.

The Seminole War was waged between the United States and the Seminole of Florida. Osceola, a Seminole leader, was killed in 1838. After five years of swamp fighting, the war finally ended and most of the five thousand Seminole were removed to the West. But some Seminole hid out in the swamps in places where white soldiers could not reach them. The descendants of those Seminole continue to live in Florida today on various small reservations.

1837 A.D.

Smallpox and other European diseases to which Indians had no immunity swept through Indian lands, killing 33 percent of the Hidatsa, 50 percent of the Arikara, and 98 percent of the Mandan populations. Only one hundred twenty-five Mandan survived the epidemics.

1839–42 A.D.

Maya ruins, buried and forgotten in the jungles of Central America since the Spanish conquests in the sixteenth century, were discovered and given world-wide publicity by American diplomat and attorney John Lloyd Stephens and British topographical artist and architect Frederick Catherwood, who published two sets of books on their adventures in Mesoamerica. Stephens and Catherwood were the first white men to give the Maya credit for the construction of their ceremonial centers, which for centuries had been attributed to the Lost Tribes of Israel, people from Atlantis and Mu, Egyptian mariners, etc. Stephens and Catherwood are usually credited with starting the study of Maya archaeology.

A mysterious stele of Copán.

Photograph by the author

1841 A.D.

The Russians cleared out of California, turning Fort Ross over to the Mexicans, who dominated most of the Far West until 1848.

1848–54 A.D.

The United States added the American Southwest and California to its possessions after a war with Mexico, and federal Indian policy was extended to those regions where Mexican rule was broken.

1849 A.D.

The Bureau of Indian Affairs was transferred from the War Department to the Department of the Interior, which it remains part of today.

1849 A.D.

The discovery of gold in California brought about the destruction of many of the Indians of California. In the 1850s the tribes were coerced into signing several treaties with the United States; by the provisions of these treaties the Indians ceded half the state to the United States in return for perpetual ownership of about eight million acres of land. The Senate, under pressure from California settlers, refused to ratify the treaties, which were tucked away in files and not rediscovered until 1905. Meanwhile, however, the Indians gave up their lands, while the eight million acres promised to them in perpetuity were sold to whites. The California Indian population subsequently dwindled from one hundred twenty thousand in 1849 to fewer than twenty thousand by 1880.

c. 1850 A.D.

Navajo silverwork is one of the most famous crafts of the American Indians, but it was not native to the Navajo. During the first half of the nineteenth century, the Navajo got some brass and copper ornaments through trade and war, and subsequently Mexican smiths taught them to work iron. Not until 1870 did the Navajo begin to copy Mexican silver techniques and begin producing their own unique silver ornaments. The Zuñi Indians learned silver techniques from the Navajo in 1872, and the Hopi borrowed techniques from the Zuñi in 1898. Each of these three tribes devised distinctive styles in the creation of jewelry.

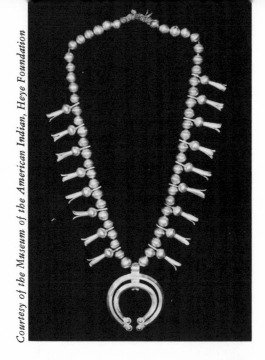

A Navajo silver squash-blossom necklace.

1853–57 A.D.

The United States acquired one hundred fifty-seven million acres of Indian land through fifty-two different treaties—all of which were subsequently broken by white Americans.

1862 A.D.

The Sioux Indians staged an uprising in Minnesota; afterward, they were forced to flee westward to the Dakotas. The Indians, led by Chief Little Crow, killed about a thousand white settlers. About thirty-eight Indians were hanged for their participation in the uprising.

1863–64 A.D.

Kit Carson, an army scout and Indian fighter, led a group of soldiers in a campaign against the Navajo of the southwestern United States to enforce the peace treaty that had been signed in 1849. (In this treaty the Navajo had acknowledged the sovereignty of the United States.) The army destroyed the sheep, the crops, and the precious fruit trees of the Navajo. Kit Carson and his men rounded up the Indians as they went and herded them eastward to Fort Sumner, which was at Bosque Redondo, New Mexico, three hundred fifty miles away. The Navajo trek to Fort Sumner came to be known as "The Long Walk."

Courtesy of the Navajo Community College Press, Many Farms, Arizona

Navajo artist Raymond Johnson's "The Long Walk."

In 1868 the prisoners of Fort Sumner were assigned a reservation in Arizona. Author LaVan Martineau believes that he has deciphered a rock painting in the Canyon de Chelly, Arizona, that tells the story of the raids of Kit Carson from the Indian viewpoint.

The Navajo record of Kit Carson's 1863–64 campaign.

Courtesy of LaVan Martineau, KC Publications

1864 A.D.

Indians were accepted as competent witnesses and under federal law were allowed to testify in trials against white men. This meant that for the first time Indians were permitted to defend themselves when they were accused of crimes.

1864 A.D.

Colonel John Chivington and his troops attacked a group of Cheyenne Indians camped on Sand Creek in Colorado (where they were living under the protection of the United States government). About one hundred fifty Indians, mostly women and children, were killed in the massacre. Although the public and a congressional committee demanded the punishment of Colonel Chivington and the troops responsible for the massacre, no action was ever taken by the army against the offenders. Therefore, some sixteen hundred Arapaho, Cheyenne, and Sioux warriors retaliated the next year, killing more people than Chivington had killed at Sand Creek.

c. 1865 A.D.

Indians had been using strings of wampum as money for hundreds of years, and by this date it had also become the most prominent basis of exchange between Indians and white men. Wampum, made by Iroquois and northeastern Algonquian tribes, consisted of white and purple beads ground from the shells of the hard-shell clam, or quahog. The Dutch began to manufacture wampum soon after settling Manhattan, and for years it was mass produced—a small factory in New Jersey made wampum well into the twentieth century. Wampum was often woven into ceremonial belts, especially by the Iroquois, and exchanged at peace parties. Wampum also has an important ritual significance to the Iroquois.

1867 A.D.

Alaska was acquired from Imperial Russia by the United States of America. It was populated by an estimated twenty-nine thousand Inuit (Eskimo), Indians, and Aleut, and about a thousand white people. A peace commission was appointed by the federal government to bring an end to warfare between Indians and white people of the area.

1868 A.D.

Chief Red Cloud of the Oglala Sioux signed a treaty in April and chose for his people a reservation on White Clay Creek in South Dakota. Indian artist Amos Bad Heart Bull painted a scene showing Chief Red Cloud with two other Indian leaders—Spotted Tail and Young Man Afraid of His Horses—during peace talks held in the Black Hills of the Dakotas with men from the Bureau of Indian Affairs.

Courtesy of Professor Hubert Alexander

1868 A.D.

The Navajo Indian reservation was created by treaty—the only reservation in the Southwest created by such legal means. It is today the largest Indian reservation in the United States. During the same year, the three-hundred-seventieth and last treaty (until the 1970s) between the United States and an Indian tribe was signed with the Nez Perces on August 13.

1868 A.D.

The U. S. Commissioner of Indian Affairs estimated that the cost to the government in the wars raging on the western plains was running at one million dollars per Indian killed.

1870 A.D.

President Ulysses S. Grant gave control of Indian agencies (government offices) on reservations to various Christian denominations after Congress passed a law prohibiting army officers (who were largely anti-Indian) from being Indian agents. (The agent's job was to administer a reservation and act as liaison between the government and the Indians on the reservation.)

1873–74 A.D.

A last stand, known as the "Buffalo War," was taken against white hunters in Oklahoma and Texas by the Cheyenne, Arapaho, Comanche, and Kiowa tribes in an attempt to save the few remaining buffalo herds in the region. A Comanche painting (on deerskin) of the period depicts the unsuccessful assault by seven hundred

A scene from the "Buffalo War."

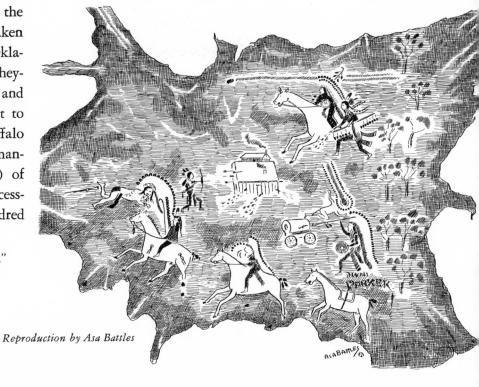

Reproduction by Asa Battles

Indians on twenty-eight buffalo hunters and merchants at the Texas settlement of Adobe.

1875 A.D.

On April 28, a group of seventy-two Kiowa and Cheyenne Indians—identified as ringleaders in raids against whites—were rounded up at Fort Sill, Oklahoma, and taken on a twenty-four-day journey by wagon and railroad to Fort Marion in St. Augustine, Florida. Provided with crayons, pencils, and paper, the Indian prisoners produced the first major Indian artworks using the white man's media.

Two scenes of prison life at Fort Marion, by Zo-Tom.

Collection of Mrs. Thomas Curtin; courtesy of Northland Press

1876 A.D.

General George A. Custer and about two hundred fifty soldiers of the U.S. Seventh Cavalry were killed on June 25 when they attacked a large hunting camp of Sioux, Cheyenne, and Arapaho Indians on the Little Big Horn River in the territory of Montana. The Indians were led by chiefs Sitting Bull, Crazy Horse, and Gall. In the fall, the United States government confiscated the Black Hills area of the Sioux reservation—in violation of the treaty of 1868.

Photograph by the author

The Indian artist Kills Two depicts a symbolic confrontation between Custer and Crazy Horse.

1877 A.D.

Chief Joseph and the Nez Perces Indians of Oregon lost their war with the United States. The Indians under Chief Joseph made a remarkable twelve-hundred-mile retreat only to surrender about thirty miles from the safety of the Canadian border. The Indians were temporarily exiled to Oklahoma. Chief Joseph said, "Hear me, my chiefs. I have fought, but from where the sun now stands, Joseph will fight no more forever."

1879 A.D.

Captain Richard Pratt, who had supervised the prisoners of Fort Marion, Florida, and provided them with art materials, opened the Carlisle Indian School in Pennsylvania. Pratt, a well-meaning and unyielding assimilationist, wanted to stamp all Indian cultural traits out of Indians. The founding of his school marked the birth of the Indian boarding school system that has taken Indian children away from their families, tribes, and cultures. The system continues to operate today.

In 1905 the Carlisle Indian School enrolled one thousand students. It closed in 1918. Its major purpose was to teach Indians how to farm, cook, sew, and do laundry and housework.

Two studies of an Indian youth—before and after his indoctrination in the white man's ways.

Courtesy of the Cumberland County Historical Society, Carlisle, Pennsylvania

1886 A.D.

The Chiricauhua Apache leader, Geronimo, surrendered in September and made peace for the final time, effectively bringing pre-twentieth-century Indian rebellion in the United States to a close.

1887 A.D.

The General Allotment Act, also known as the Dawes Act, was passed by Congress. It provided for the division of tribally held Indian lands into severalty —that is, the lands would henceforth be owned by individual Indians rather than by tribes, whether tribal leaders consented or not. The idea behind the act was to assimilate Indians by making them accept the non-Indian idea of the private ownership of property—a concept totally alien to Indians. One result of the act was the reduction in Indian-owned lands from one hundred thirty-eight million acres in 1887 to forty-eight million acres when allotment finally ceased, in 1934, under the Wheeler–Howard Act.

1890 A.D.

The Ghost Dance Movement led by Wovoka, a Paiute holy man and prophet, gained its greatest influence among the Indians of the western plains. Wovoka foretold the restoration of the Indian, the return of the buffalo, and the disappearance of white men from America. He envisioned a vast railroad train that, announced by an explosion, would roll into view carrying all the dead Indians who would live again, and all the buffalo. These events, Wovoka said, would be brought about by a return to Indian customs and by the performance of a "ghost dance" that had been revealed to him in a vision. Many of the larger Plains tribes sent delegations to Wovoka to bring back details of his teachings. Followers of the Ghost Dance Movement wore characteristic "ghost

Courtesy of the University of Nebraska Press

Amos Bad Heart Bull drew this picture of the death of Sitting Bull and his son, Crow Foot, who was killed in his sleep. These assassinations led to the Ghost Dance fanaticism of Wounded Knee.

shirts" and "ghost dresses" that were painted with iconography that was believed by some to be bulletproof.

On December 29, a group of three hundred Sioux Indians under Chief Big Foot, en route to a Ghost Dance encampment, were massacred at Wounded Knee Creek, South Dakota, by the U.S. Seventh Cavalry—despite the fact that the Indians were unarmed and were involved in a religious pilgrimage. For many Indians, particularly those of the Great Plains, this failure of their religion brought about all loss of hope of spiritually defeating the white man.

Photograph by the author

A "ghost shirt."

1900 A.D.

The Indian population of the United States was shown to have declined by more than eleven thousand people in the ten years since 1890.

c. 1900 A.D.

J. W. Fewkes, an ethnologist working with the Hopi Indians in Arizona, commissioned a group of anonymous self-trained artists to depict the kachinas of Hopi ceremonial life. Using crayons and paper for the first time, these Hopi men made drawings that are among the first produced in the Southwest using the white man's media. Fewkes also inspired the famed potter Nampeyo to resurrect the nearly lost style of Sikyatki pottery.

From Fewkes, Hopi Kachinas Drawn by Native Artists

TAWA

One of the drawings of Hopi kachinas commissioned by J. W. Fewkes.

1918 A.D.

A peyote cult came to Indians in the United States from Mexico, and it was militantly embraced by the Comanche chief Quanah Parker despite strong legal efforts by the Bureau of Indian Affairs to outlaw the use of the drug. Eventually the famous hallucinogenic cactus "button" was made the center of a vision-quest religion called the Native American Church. The church was incorporated in Oklahoma on October 10 by members of the Ponca, Cheyenne, Comanche, Oto, Kiowa, and Apache tribes.

Courtesy of the Museum of the American Indian, Heye Foundation

A picture of a Kickapoo peyote ceremony by Shawnee artist Ernest Spybuck.

1922 A.D.

For the first time since their revolt against the Spaniards in 1680, the Pueblo Indians of New Mexico united. They formed the All Pueblo Council; its aim was to defeat the Bursum Bill, pending before Congress, which would have given white squatters the right to claim Pueblo lands.

1924 A.D.

American citizenship was bestowed on all native-born United States Indians who had not already attained citizenship status. This ruling was apparently made because so many American Indians had fought and died in World War I without the advantage of being citizens of the land of their ancestors.

1933 A.D.

John Collier was appointed Commissioner of Indian Affairs to administer the "New Deal" for Indians. In many ways a sympathetic man of highly artistic insights, Collier might also be seen as a perpetuator of the false notion of the "noble savage."

1934 A.D.

The Wheeler–Howard Indian Reorganization Act and the Johnson–O'Malley Act were passed by Congress, and the federal policy of forced assimilation of Indians that had characterized the preceding fifty years was officially reversed. Now tribes were permitted to retain Indian land rather than having it allotted to individual Indians (who could then sell it to non-Indians). The tribes were also encouraged to adopt constitutions modeled after the American one, and to implement self-government. Though it was highly effective in reversing many of the laws that had destroyed Indian tribal authority and culture, the Reorganization Act has also been cited as the basis for many of the subsequent inequities in the existence of Indians in America.

1944 A.D.

The National Congress of American Indians was organized in Denver. It was the first effective national Indian association in the United States.

1946 A.D.

William Brophy replaced John Collier as Commissioner of Indian Affairs. Congress created the Indian Claims Commission to settle Indian claims against the United States. Many Indians saw this commission as a contradiction, since it seemed unreasonable to believe that a United States agency could process Indian claims against the United States without a conflict of interest. At about the same time, the Indian artist Beatien Yazz (Jimmie Toddy) painted a picture showing a small western town's exploitation of Indian culture as a tourist attraction. Indians have been offended by the white man's attempts to turn them into entertainers ever since 1900, when Indians were first hired by Wild West shows and expositions. In the painting, artist Yazz offers an early expression of Indian political irony; a sign in the shop window reads NO INDIANS ALLOWED.

Painting by Beatien Yazz courtesy of Mrs. Sally Wagner

1948 A.D.

Arizona and New Mexico became the last states to give Indians the right to vote in non-Indian elections.

1953 A.D.

Special federal liquor prohibition laws relating to Indians were repealed. Public Law 280 gave states the right to assume responsibility for law and order on Indian reservations—a concept hotly contested by Indians until partial repeal of the law was signed in 1968 with the Indian Civil Rights Bill.

Courtesy of the Tribal Arts Gallery, Oklahoma City

"Indian Bar,"
by Comanche artist
Rance Hood.

1954 A.D.

Congress passed laws to bring about the termination of federal responsibility to the Menominee Reservation in Wisconsin and the Klamath Reservation in Oregon. The laws meant that the Menominee and Klamath suddenly had no protection under laws that defined the rights of Indians on reservations.

1955 A.D.

The Public Health Service assumed responsibility for Indian health and medical care. It took over this role from the Bureau of Indian Affairs.

1968 A.D.

The Indian Civil Rights Act, extending the provisions of the Bill of Rights to reservation Indians—whether they wanted those rights or not—became law. The act also stated that Indian consent had to be gained before states could assume law-and-order jurisdiction on reservations—a provision that finally returned jurisdiction over Indian law to Indians.

1968 A.D.

The American Indian Movement (A.I.M.) was founded on July 29 in Minneapolis, Minnesota, to deal with the problems faced by relocated urban Indians in the United States.

On October 30, 1972, about five hundred Indians staged a protest demonstration called "The Trail of Broken Treaties."

Courtesy of the American Indian Press Association

1968 A.D.

About forty-one Mohawk attempted to block the St. Lawrence Seaway International Bridge to protest the Canadian government's failure to honor the Jay Treaty of 1794, which guaranteed the Mohawk the right to travel unrestricted between the United States and Canada. They were arrested by Canadian police but were later released without being charged. Since this event, the border-crossing rights of the Mohawk have been honored by Canada—in fact, all native Americans are now allowed to cross the border whenever they wish. This has been especially important in the eastern part of the country, where many tribes have lands on both sides of the border.

1969 A.D.

Indians invaded Alcatraz Island in San Francisco Bay, California, and occupied it as a demonstration of their mistreatment as Indians. The occupation made many Americans aware, for the first time, that Indians had strong grievances against the United States. It also brought the fact that Indians were "real people with real problems" into focus for the vast majority of people around the world, who had simply taken it for granted that Indians who were not totally assimilated into American culture were extinct.

From the beginning, Indian militancy has been concerned with the problems of landless, urban Indians whose circumstances are desperate, rather than with Indians enrolled on reservations and provided rights as Indians under federal laws.

1970 A.D.

The American Indian population had increased by more than 50 percent since 1960 and totaled 791,839, the U.S. Census Bureau reported in April. The Census Bureau listed Indian population in cities as follows:

Los Angeles, California	24,509	Phoenix, Arizona	11,159
Tulsa, Oklahoma	15,519	Minneapolis, Minnesota	9,852
Oklahoma City, Oklahoma	13,033	Seattle, Washington	9,496
San Francisco, California	12,011	Chicago, Illinois	8,996
New York, New York	12,000	Tucson, Arizona	8,837

At about the time of the 1970 census, a young Cree Indian painter named Alfred Young Man painted a vivid and ironic expression of the relationship of Indians to non-Indians; it is called "Six White Men and One Indian."

Painting by Alfred Young Man courtesy of the artist

1970 A.D.

The Canadian government issued a "white paper" on Indian affairs that leaned toward the termination of special Indian status and benefits as derived from various treaties. President Nixon of the United States formulated a policy of "self-determination" for Indian tribes that was clearly an effort to end federal responsibility to Indians.

1971 A.D.

In June, federal marshals removed the last of the Indians who had occupied Alcatraz Island since 1969.

1972 A.D.

The Bureau of Indian Affairs headquarters in Washington, D.C., were occupied by militant Indians from November 2 through November 8. About five hundred Indians led by Dennis Banks and Russell Means had protested in a demonstration called "The Trail of Broken Treaties" on October 30. This action apparently led to the mood of Indian outrage that motivated the takeover of the B.I.A. offices.

1973 A.D.

Approximately two hundred armed Oglala Sioux and members of the American Indian Movement, led by Russell Means and Dennis Banks, occupied the Pine Ridge, South Dakota, reservation hamlet called Wounded Knee from February 27 to May 8, demanding a change of elected tribal leaders, a review of all Indian treaties, and a full-scale U.S. Senate investigation of the treatment of Indians. The Indians, who called themselves "the Independent Oglala Sioux Nation," were surrounded by federal marshals. A state of siege resulted during which negotiations alternated with gunfire on both sides. The event, which the media cynically viewed as more theatrical than political, nonetheless drew international sympathy for the Indian cause. When the Indians surrendered their weapons and evacuated Wounded Knee (in exchange for a written promise of negotiations on Indian grievances by five representatives appointed by the President), two Indians had been killed and one federal marshal seriously wounded.

There has been significant evidence since the occupation of Wounded Knee that militant Indians are being harassed and subjected to an invasion of privacy by law enforcement agencies. Though there has been criticism of the militant Indians by elected officers of Indian reservations, most Indians accept the general purposes of A.I.M. as important ones, even if they do not approve of the organization's methods. Nevertheless, reservation Indians have often objected to the fact that self-appointed militant Indian leaders have gotten more attention and have had more discussion with government officials than elected reservation officials. There is also criticism of A.I.M. for the apparent theft and destruction of Indian art and artifacts that were on exhibition at the B.I.A. offices when they were occupied in November, 1972.

Drawing by Asa Battles

Fritz Scholder's
"Super Indian No. 2."

Courtesy of Susan T. Aberbach and Joachim Jean Aberbach

During the several years since the occupation of Wounded Knee, there has been a complex interaction between militant Indians and elected Indian officers on reservations, traditional Indians, and semi-assimilated urban Indians, as well as between the government and the Indian community. In January, 1974, the first trial stemming from the seventy-one-day occupation of Wounded Knee began at the Federal Court Building in St. Paul, Minnesota. The appearance of Indians in traditional braids and jewelry, wearing sunglasses and riding motorcycles, has become a common image—one perfectly expressing the conflict of a people living between two cultures. Mission Indian painter Fritz Scholder of California has depicted the irony of the contemporary Indian predicament in his internationally acclaimed paintings. Scholder's art, which uses the techniques of contemporary art in combination with traditional Indian iconography, rests on the brink of the same transitional moment that Indians find themselves in at the end of the twentieth century. "Super Indian

No. 2" sums up the paradoxical world of modern Indians. In the black comedy of this painting there is an equal expression of irony and pathos. There is also irony in the confusion most white Americans feel about Indians. They suspect that, like other minorities, Indians are staging demonstrations and issuing proclamations in an effort to attain equality and to get their "fair share." But it is an error to attribute to Indians the hopes and aspirations of other national and racial groups. As we have seen, throughout his history the Indian had one central motive and, no matter how complex the contemporary situation and its many problems, that Indian motive remains central: the American Indian wishes to control his own destiny, and to find his own way into the twentieth century. He wants the fruits of the promises made to him—promises in exchange for which he surrendered the vast land he once occupied. He wants to live in his own world. He wants to perpetuate his own culture. He wants to be Indian.

SELECTED BIBLIOGRAPHY

Baldwin, Gordon C. *America's Buried Past: The Story of North American Archaeology.* New York: G. P. Putnam's Sons, 1962.

Brandon, William, ed. *The American Heritage Book of Indians.* New York: Dell Publishing Co., 1961.

Bushnell, G. H. S. *The First Americans.* New York: McGraw-Hill Book Co., 1968.

Ceram, C. W. *The First American: A Story of North American Archaeology.* New York: Harcourt Brace Jovanovich, 1971.

Collier, John. *Indians of the Americas.* New York: W. W. Norton & Co., 1947.

Dockstader, Frederick J. *Indian Art in America: The Arts and Crafts of the North American Indian.* Greenwich, Conn.: New York Graphic Society, 1967.

Driver, Harold E. *Indians of North America.* 2d rev. ed. Chicago: University of Chicago Press, 1969.

Eggan, Fred. *The American Indian: Perspectives for the Study of Social Change.* Chicago: University of Chicago Press, 1966.

Farb, Peter. *Man's Rise to Civilization as Shown by the Indians of North America from Primeval Times to the Coming of the Industrial State.* New York: E. P. Dutton & Co., 1968.

Gorenstein, Shirley, et al. *North America.* New York: St. Martin's Press, 1975.

Hester, Joseph A., Jr., and MacGawan, Kenneth. *Early Man in the New World.* New York: Peter Smith, 1962.

Highwater, Jamake. *Anpao: An American Indian Odyssey.* Philadelphia and New York: J. B. Lippincott Co., 1977.

———. *Fodor's Indian America.* New York: David McKay Co., 1975.

———. *Ritual of the Wind: American Indian Ceremonies, Music, and Dances.* New York: Viking Press, 1977.

———. *Song from the Earth: American Indian Painting.* Boston: New York Graphic Society, 1976.

Irvine, Keith, ed. *Encyclopedia of Indians of the Americas.* St. Clair Shores, Mich.: Scholarly Press, 1974.

Jennings, Jesse D. *Prehistory of North America.* 2d ed. New York: McGraw-Hill Book Co., 1974.

Josephy, Alvin M., Jr. *The Indian Heritage of America.* New York: Alfred A. Knopf, 1968.

La Farge, Oliver. *A Pictorial History of the American Indian.* Rev. ed. New York: Crown Publishers, 1974.

Martin, Paul S., et al. *Indians Before Columbus: Twenty Thousand Years of North American History Revealed by Archaeology.* Chicago: University of Chicago Press, 1947.

Morgan, Lewis H. *Houses and House Life of the American Aborigines.* Chicago: University of Chicago Press, 1966.

National Geographic Society. *The World of the American Indian.* Washington, D.C.: National Geographic Society, 1974.

Oswalt, Wendell H. *This Land Was Theirs: A Study of the North American Indian.* 2d ed. New York: John Wiley & Sons, 1973.

Owen, Roger C., et al. *The North American Indians: A Sourcebook.* New York: Macmillan Co., 1967.

Sanders, William T., and Marino, Joseph P. *New World Prehistory: Archaeology of the American Indian.* Englewood Cliffs, N.J.: Prentice-Hall, 1971.

Sellards, Elias H. *Early Man in America: A Study in Prehistory.* Austin, Tex.: University of Texas Press, 1952.

Silverberg, Robert. *Mound Builders of Ancient America: The Archaeology of a Myth.* Greenwich, Conn.: New York Graphic Society, 1968.

Snow, Dean. *The Archaeology of North America.* New York: Viking Press, 1976.

Spencer, Robert F., et al. *The Native Americans.* New York: Harper & Row, 1965.

Underhill, Ruth M. *Red Man's America: A History of the Indians in the United States.* Rev. ed. Chicago: University of Chicago Press, 1971.

Willey, Gordon R. *An Introduction to American Archaeology: Volume 1, North and Middle America.* Englewood Cliffs, N.J.: Prentice-Hall, 1966.

Willey, Gordon R., and Sabloff, Jeremy A. *A History of American Archaeology.* San Francisco: W. H. Freeman & Co., 1974.

Wormington, H. M. *Ancient Man in North America.* 4th rev. ed. Denver: Denver Museum of Natural History, 1957.

INDEX

Timeline chart — A.D. (top/right panel)

DATES	MIDDLE AMERICA	THE WEST	THE EAST	THE NORTH	OLD WORLD
1600	SPANISH CONQUEST BEGINS WITH CORTES	CORONADO EXPLORES SOUTHWEST	DE SOTO EXPEDITION CROSSES SOUTHEAST	HUDSON SEARCHES FOR NORTHWEST PASSAGE	SHAKESPEARE
1500					MAGELLAN; COLUMBUS
1400	AZTEC CULTURE AT HEIGHT	ANASAZI ABANDON FOUR CORNERS AREA	SOUTHERN CULT. HIGHEST EXPRESSION OF CEREMONIAL ART IN TEMPLE MOUND PERIOD		GUTENBERG PRINTING PROCESS
1300					MARCO POLO
1200	TOLTEC CULTURE				MAGNA CARTA
1100				THULE ESKIMO MIGRATION TO EASTERN CANADA AND GREENLAND	
1000			EXPANSION OF MISSISSIPPIAN CULTURE	NORSE VOYAGES TO VINLAND	NORMAN CONQUEST OF ENGLAND
900	ZENITH OF CLASSIC MAYA CIVILIZATION	ANASAZI AND HOHOKAM CULTURES FLOURISH IN SOUTHWEST			
800			TEMPLE MOUND PERIOD BEGINS		CHARLEMAGNE
700			REGIONAL CULTURES THRIVE AFTER DECLINE OF HOPEWELL		MOSLEMS INVADE SPAIN
600					MOHAMMED
500		HUNTERS, FISHERMEN, AND GATHERERS INHABIT CALIFORNIA AND NORTHWEST COAST			
400	TEOTIHUACÁN AT HEIGHT		HOPEWELL CULTURE REPLACES ADENA		FALL OF ROME
300		MOGOLLON AND HOHOKAM CULTURES			CONSTANTINE
200					
100					
A.D.					BIRTH OF CHRIST

Timeline chart — B.C. (bottom/left panel)

DATES	MIDDLE AMERICA	THE WEST	THE EAST	THE NORTH	OLD WORLD
B.C. 100		POTTERY AND AGRICULTURE BEGIN IN SOUTHWEST AS DESERT CULTURE CONTINUES IN GREAT BASIN			HAN DYNASTY, CHINA
200					
300					ALEXANDER
400				POTTERY FRAGMENT, CAPE DENBIGH, ALASKA	
500					PERICLES
600			BURIAL MOUND PERIOD—AND POSSIBLY SOME AGRICULTURE—BEGIN WITH ADENA CULTURE	FIRST POTTERY IN ARCTIC	CONFUCIUS; BUDDHA; HOMER
700					
800			EFFIGY PIPE, ADENA, OHIO		CHOU DYNASTY, CHINA; SHANG DYNASTY, CHINA; STONEHENGE; TUTANKHAMEN
900	OLMEC CULTURE				
1000				BEGINNING OF ESKIMO CULTURE	
2000	FIRST POTTERY	REED DECOY, LOVELOCK CAVE, NEVADA	N. AMERICA'S EARLIEST POTTERY APPEARS ALONG S. ATLANTIC COAST		PYRAMIDS AT GIZA
3000			BIG GAME HUNTING CULTURE ENDS ON PLAINS	HARPOON POINT, CAPE DENBIGH, ALASKA	MENES, FIRST PHARAOH OF EGYPT
4000	MAIZE CULTIVATED IN TEHUACAN VALLEY			ARCTIC SMALL TOOL CULTURE	
5000		MILLING STONE, DANGER CAVE, UTAH	EDEN POINT, FINLEY, WYOMING		
6000			DIVERSIFICATION OF EASTERN ARCHAIC CULTURES	NORTHWEST MICROBLADE CULTURE	
7000		DESERT CULTURE; HUNTING AND GATHERING BEGIN		HARDAWAY POINT, HARDAWAY, N.C.	
8000			FOLSOM POINT, LINDENMEIER, COLORADO		AGRICULTURE IN MIDDLE EAST
9000			PALEO-INDIAN HUNTERS OF ICE AGE MAMMALS THROUGHOUT N. AMERICA		
10,000					
11,000		MAN ENTERS THE AMERICAS ACROSS THE BERING LAND BRIDGE BEFORE 10,000 B.C.			
12,000					
13,000					
14,000					LASCAUX CAVE, FRANCE
15,000					

Drawn by Asa Battles

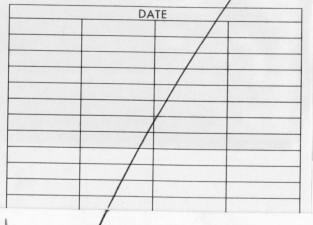